Karen

ACCOLADES FOR MINDSET CHANGE FOR COMMUNITY TRANSFORMATION

The book *Mindset Change For Community Transformation*, by Bishop Titus Masika, is a must-read for those involved in development work in Africa. The author has brought to light what many development actors may have overlooked either due to the sin of commission, omission or just pure ignorance. It is amazing that within a short period of about five years, and without much reliance on donor support, the Yatta community has managed to embrace a mindset development philosophy that has transformed over 6000 families. I commend Bishop Masika for championing a mindset change development model that is enhancing community resilience to climate change and increased household income.

> **—PROF. JESSE T. NJOKA**, *Associate Professor of Range Management, Department of Land Resources Management and Agricultural Technology; Acting Director, African Dryland Institute for Sustainability at the University of Nairobi*

Bishop Masika has demonstrated in Yatta that poverty is primarily a mindset; families that were living in a water-stressed context have learned to conserve this limited resource for food security. Poverty is at the same time broken relationships; those who have minimal land in Yatta have been able to create wealth together by working together. Finally, poverty in Africa is ultimately spiritual; the fear of witchcraft divides family, communities and nations. By engaging with the power of Jesus

Christ who overcame Satan on the cross, Bishop Masika is discipling the nations.

> **—REV. DENNIS TONGOI,** *CMS-Africa*
> *International Director*

Bishop Dr. Titus Masika, in this book, invites us to challenge ourselves and our communities from a sense of apathetic nonchalance (indifference) towards our ability to create wealth and reinvent communities. The greatest challenge of life is tempered with a resolve modeled on the Christian ethics of hard work and positive thinking. It is a book anyone who is interested in real people's development should not only read, but also treat as a guide to effective community mobilisation that achieves sustainable livelihoods for a people. It is an easy read and step by step capacity building treatise for every reader and learner.

> **—PROF. KIVUTHA KIBWANA,** *Governor, Makueni County*

Bishop Titus Masika has begun a revolution in the small community of Yatta, in Machakos County; a revolution against traditional models of community development that have absorbed hundreds of billions of dollars but have failed to address the most fundamental causes of poverty in Africa. Through the Operation Mwolyo Out (OMO) initiative, Bishop Masika provides a practical demonstration of the power of the mind to imprison and to liberate. Change a man's mindset and you change the direction of his life. This book *Mindset Change For Community Transformation* is a long overdue presentation of

Bishop Masika's insights on why an obscure, poverty stricken community in Eastern Kenya is making waves in development circles around the world.

> **—PETE ONDENG,** *Director, Lead Africa Institute*

In the three decades my husband and I have known Reverend Agnes and Bishop Titus Masika, we have experienced the love of God in the way we have fellowshipped, ministered to others by partnering in evangelism and mobilizing communities to turn their lives to Christ. We have been to Embu, Busia, Hola, Bungoma and even Taita Taveta to spread the liberating news of a risen Christ.

In the early days of Christian Impact Mission, when it was first revealed to us the need to match the gospel message with practical Christianity, I became the Chairperson of what was to become one of the most inspiring projects I have ever been involved in. Together with my husband, Engineer Reverend Sospeter Mbogo, we gave the effort our all and watched in awe as God's faithfulness shone through the transformed lives we witnessed in Yatta – a hitherto arid land of death and despair.

Mindset Change For Community Transformation is a great resource book for missionary work, community development and the Church. May Reverend Dr. Steven Kanya, current Chairman, steer CIM to greater heights as it emerges as a model for mind transformation and practical Christianity in Africa.

> **—REV. CANON ROSEMARY MBOGO,** *Provincial Secretary*, Anglican Church of Kenya

MINDSET CHANGE
For COMMUNITY
TRANSFORMATION

MINDSET CHANGE
For COMMUNITY
TRANSFORMATION

BISHOP TITUS MASIKA

Copyright © 2016 Bishop Titus Masika
ISBN: 978-9966-1788-6-2

All rights reserved

No part of this publication may be reproduced, distributed, or transmitted in any form or by any means, or stored in any database or retrieval system, without the prior written permission of the author and Sahel Publishing Association.

The author assumes full responsibility for all content of this book

All Scripture quotations, unless otherwise indicated, are taken from King James Version (KJV)

Published by Sahel Publishing Association,
a subsidiary of Sahel Books Inc.
P.O. Box 21232 – 00505
Nairobi, Kenya
Tel: +011-254-715-596-106
For questions and orders log on to:
www.sahelpublishing.net

A Sahel Book
Nairobi. New Delhi. London. Nashville.
Editor: Sam Okello
Interior and cover design by: Hellen Wahonya Okello
Printed in India

To Emmanuel Masika Gor, Gabrielle Tiany Gor,
Ranise Gatheru Muguro, Tevita Gitonga Muguro and
Hawi Wema Gor, my grandchildren for whom
I look to the future with hope

FOREWORD 2015

Every successful organisation has a story – a narrative of milestones that provide a guiding inspiration, identity, ethos and values for future generations of employees.

Our first leadership team visit to Yatta in June 2012 disrupted our story. It was a watershed event that fundamentally shifted what was to become the future narrative of our story in World Vision Tanzania. We were profoundly challenged by the deep transformation we found among previously impoverished people who had barely eked out an existence in the arid landscape of Yatta.

This community had broken free from the poverty chains of powerlessness and dependency upon external aid. They were empowered to chart their own destiny: providing for children, building community, building a future. They had become stewards of the creative freedom God placed inside each person and the natural resources he placed all around them.

These communities found their developmental footing without external donor funding. In fact they were highly skeptical of aid agencies and the perceived tyranny of agendas, values and conditionalities set in capital cities on the other side of the world. Their previous experience with such organizations had stripped them of their dignity and their destiny – inadvertently of course, by fostering a state of dependence on external assistance.

We came away from that encounter with a renewed understanding that the foundation of transformational development has very little to do with the transfer of external resources, capacity building and technologies into impoverished communities. It had a lot to do with mind-set change at the individual level. We learned this change began with the individual then moved outward to the family and then to the community.

The result was a community with the belief it had the resources and the will to drive its own development agenda. Personal transformation was foundational to social and economic change. While perhaps this should be no surprise, the sheer scale of wealth creation accomplished by these communities formerly depending on annual, dry season, food aid hand-outs overwhelmed us.

Even more impressive were the underlying Christian values evident in the community. The full capacity and potential of both men and women had been unleashed to further development in the family and in the community. Children were well nourished, well cared for and in school. There was no public loitering or drunkenness and no theft of farming tools or produce left in the field. Everyone seemed to be proactively engaged in productive activities. We had to admit this scale of sustainable transformation is rarely witnessed among development practitioners in Sub Saharan Africa.

Upon our return to Tanzania we met with all of our senior managers, shared our experience and together forged a sort of manifesto declaring that World Vision Tanzania would pursue a socio-economic empowerment approach to development. Our first action was to engage in a massive change management process. We wanted to ensure that all our staff were agents of empowerment and transformation, neither inadvertently bringing nor entrenching a dependency mind-set into the communities.

It has been a dance of discovery. We move forward, sideways and backwards in pursuit of catalyzing sustainable, agriculturally based enterprise movements that will support 'life in all its fullness' for children and their families.

In the three and half years since that first visit we have seen remarkable transformation evidenced by household initiated digging of over 1,600 water pans, formation of over 3,800 savings groups which provide loan capital to more than 1,300 farming producer groups. These producer groups are consolidated into more than 280 cooperative-like commercial villages participating in value chain development, collective bargaining and profitable market linkages.

If you are interested in understanding an approach to community transformation that works, this book is for you.

If you have ever been frustrated by development contexts that do not respond well to planning and execution strategies alone, this book is for you.

If you have ever been baffled by communities that simply do not want their girls to be educated, do not like the taste of clean water, refuse immunizations, do not value the protection of their children, do not accept gender equity, are not interested to work, fear the retribution of evil spirits or curses if they try to improve their lot in life - the list goes on and on – this book is for you.

If you are a government or development actor and want to learn how you or your institution can become a catalyst for appropriately channeling aid into community priorities and critical areas that build the community capacity to drive its own agenda, this book is for you.

> —**TIM ANDREWS,** *World Vision Tanzania, National Director. Development Practitioner – 25 years.*

FOREWORD 2015

The work that the Christian Impact Mission (CIM) Development Model has done in the Yatta area of Machakos County, Kenya, is great for one reason: it humanizes people and spurs real development. Out of a poverty stricken population, emerge a robust self-reliant community. And this within a short period of time. The book advances the CIM Development Model which employs Transformed Empowered World View and Mindset (TEWM) as opposed to the Traditional Worldview and Mindset (TWM). It offers a practitioner's insight to development from a mindset liberation point of view which challenges the traditionally held belief that "people need to be assisted/given aid for them to develop". In doing this, it exhibits the benefits of a strong ethical dimension that is faith-based through the religious institutions.

As a practitioner of community development, he and others developed and incubated the model in Yatta in Machakos County, but transplanted it to Tanzania, Rwanda, Malawi and other parts of Kenya. The model enshrines capacity building of a citizenry so that they can realise their own livelihood and investment opportunities. It has its mainstay in community governance and the holistic approach that is realized through "value-chain" of development of people and ideas. Bishop Dr. Titus Masika in this book invites us to challenge ourselves and our communities from a sense of apathetic nonchalance towards our ability to create wealth and reinvent communities. The greatest challenge of life is tempered with a resolve modeled on the Christian ethics of hard work and positive thinking.

It is a great book of transformational change which goes beyond the critical analysis and potent anger of Graham Hancock's *Lords of Poverty* and Dambisa Moyo's *Dead Aid* to recreate community, to create an ethos for development and practical orientated social re-engineering. It is a book anyone who is interested in real people's development should not only read, but also treat as a guide to effective community organizing tool to achieve sustainable livelihoods for a people and their community. It is an easy read and step by step capacity building treatise for every reader and learner.

Over 500 Makueni County government staff and other members of the community have in the recent past visited the Yatta community which has developed and embraced the CIM Development Model. We learned the invaluable lessons that are captured in this book. It has helped us as a county to begin to shift focus from the traditional facility based development practised by most governments to the people centered holistic development. This model carries the promise of a new mindset, consciousness and resolve leading to transformative visioning, planning and development praxis.

—PROF KIVUTHA KIBWANA, *Governor, Makueni County.*

TABLE OF CONTENTS

Foreword 2015 Tim Andrews	13
Foreword 2015 Prof. Kivutha Kibwana	17
List of Abbreviations and Acronyms	23
PROLOGUE	27
RETHINKING DEVELOPMENT MODELS	29
Shifting Gears	29
Yatta's Problem was Africa's Problem	33
Spiritism Gave Way to Dependency Syndrome	34
The Yatta Model	35
INTRODUCTION	40
INTO THE TRENCHES	40
Operation Mwolyo Out	43
A model to the World	45
CHAPTER 1: UNDERSTANDING DEVELOPMENT	46
Introduction	46
Corporate Social Responsibility	49
Development	50
Approach to Development	54
Contrasting Approaches of the Twin Worldviews	55
The Jesus Approach	74
No More Theory, Practical Solution Now	75

CHAPTER 2: CHANGE IN MINDSET ... 78
Margaret's Testimony ... 82
Mindset ... 84
Symbolism of Mindset and Development ... 85
The CIM Development Model ... 94
Inside the CIM development model ... 97

CHAPTER 3: WORLDVIEW – RELIGION AND DEVELOPMENT ... 100
What is Worldview? ... 102
The Greek Worldview ... 103
The Hebrew Worldview ... 103
Greek Worldview in African Institutions ... 105
Hebrew Worldview in African Institutions ... 106
What is the Christian Worldview? ... 106
A Christian Worldview of the Individual ... 108
The Challenge of Dualism ... 108
The Impact of Creating Dichotomies of Secular and of Sacred ... 109
Consequences of those Choices ... 111
Challenge of Animism ... 112
This calls for real leadership ... 116

CHAPTER 4: MOBILISATION PHILOSOPHY ... 120
Standoff at the Katutuni Shrine ... 123
So … What is Mobilisation? ... 124
Ongoing Training in Yatta ... 126
Who is to be Mobilised? ... 130
Spurred to Urgency by Death ... 136

CHAPTER 5: MOBILISATION FOR 1-ACRE-RULE MIRACLE — 138

The 1-Acre-Rule-Miracle — 142
Apportioning the 1-Acre — 144
Components of the 1-Acre-Rule Miracle — 146
Benefits of the 1-Acre-Rule Miracle — 155
Exporting the 1-Acre-Rule Miracle — 158

CHAPTER 6: GENDER IN DEVELOPMENT — 162

Gender Defined — 163
Relationship between Culture and Gender — 165
Gender and Worldviews — 168
Gender Sensitivity in Development — 169
Integrating Gender in Community Development — 170
Benefits of Integrating Gender in Community Development — 171

CHAPTER 7: SECURING OUR YOUTH — 173

Securing our Youth — 173
Our View of the Youth — 174

CHAPTER 8: SUSTAINABLE COMMUNITY SECURITY — 183

Components of Sustainable Development — 184
Key Questions in Comprehensive Community — 189
Key Elements of Comprehensive Security — 195
Dependence Syndrome or the *Mwolyo* Mentality — 198
Why We Fight Dependency — 198
Own the Problem, Own the Solution — 199
Overstretched Central Pool — 200
Aiding to Fail — 200

Competition Turned on its Head	202
Self-Esteem	203

CHAPTER 9: QUALITY ASSURANCE — 205
Elements that Define Quality	208
Quality Assurance through Lenses of Worldviews	209
Quality Assurance in the CIM Model	211

CHAPTER 10: MENTORING FOR TRANSFORMATION — 219
Defining Mentoring	221
Key Elements in Mentoring	228
Mission as a Factor in Mentoring	228
Partnership Development	230
Cultivating Prayer	230

CHAPTER 11: PREPARATION FOR RETIRMENT — 233
Key Views on Retirement	233
The Fear of Facing an Uncertain Future	237
Donor Ourselves Philosophy	238

BIBLIOGRAPHY — 241
ACKNOWLEDGEMENTS — 243
PHOTO GALLERY — 247

LIST OF ABBREVIATIONS AND ACRONYMS

ABCD	Asset Based Community Development
ASAL	Arid and Semi-Arid Lands
AUSAID	Australian Aid (Australian Agency for International Development)
BOT	Board of Trustees
CARICOM	Caribbean Community
CBOs	Community Based Organisations
CIM	Christian Impact Mission
CiM	Change in Mindset
COVACAs	Community-Owned Vulnerabilities and Capacities Assessments)
DANIDA	Danish Development Agency
EAC	East African Community
ECOWAS	Economic Community of West African States
FBOs	Faith Based Organisations
FEWSN	Famine Early Warning System Network

ICT	Information, Communication and Technology
IGA	Income Generating Activities
INGO	International Non-Governmental Organisation
JICA	Japan International Cooperation Agency
KARI	Kenya Agricultural Research Institute
M& E	Monitoring and Evaluation
Mwolyo	CIM's concept of dependency taken from Kamba word for relief food.
NGO	Non-Governmental Organisation
OAU	Organisation of African Unity, now AU (African Union)
OMO	Operation Mwolyo Out
Serikali Saidia	A Kiswahili phrase meaning, "Government Help us!" A cry for relief in which Government is seen as the solution for everything.
SADC	Southern African Development Community
SWOT	Strengths, Weaknesses, Opportunities and Threats
TEWM	Transformed Empowered Worldview and Mindset

TWM	Traditional Worldview and Mindset
USAID	United States Aid and International Development
Utongoi	CIM's concept of leadership taken from Kamba language.
WASH	Water Sanitation and Hygiene

PROLOGUE

RETHINKING DEVELOPMENT MODELS

It began in the year 2000, when the plight of the people of Yatta took centre stage in my mind. In a land of dry riverbeds, rare but torrential downpours, ruinous drunkenness and demonic ritualism, there was little to hope for and many people who had the luck to escape the horror of the troubled village never looked back. Hunger, disease, death and despair defined the village, making it one of Africa's most reliable strongholds of satanic rituals, demonic curses and human misery. For this state of affairs to change, redemption had to take place. The land was in desperate need of healing.

It was realization of this fact – which I today regard as revelation – that fired me up to question the notion of a loving God cast in the backdrop of human suffering. How was it possible that an omnipotent God, the Creator of the universe, watched helplessly as His creation suffered all over Africa, with the epicenter of agony being in Yatta? In 2000 to 2005, I reflected on these matters. I needed to understand God. I wanted to know whether this was His plan for man or something had gone terribly wrong.

As evidence began to emerge of God's love and His desire to give man nothing but happiness, I started sharing my thoughts in earnest, warning religious institutions and anyone who cared to listen that we had let God down. We had failed to live up to our calling as men and women cast in the role of bearing hope in a troubled, fallen world.

It was while in this mode that the Bible League invited me to a meeting it hosted in Nairobi. The year was 2005 and my thoughts had greatly matured as I prayerfully read the Bible. I shared those thoughts at the meeting in Nairobi.

Eric Wafukho, the then head of Christian Commitment Department in World Vision, who was in the meeting, sensed that I had an unusually radical perspective that could help liberate Africa. He had just formed Africa Leadership Ministry as a vehicle for seeking help to push for Africa's transformation. In hindsight, it couldn't have been a chance encounter; it was divine connectivity.

Together with Eric Musee, the Director of Bible League, Eric offered to host a separate meeting in which I would discuss more deeply my vision and thoughts about Africa's transformation and the role of religious institutions in it. Eric offered to be a consultant *pro bono* and walked with me through the period, documenting and advising on the development model as it evolved.

In 2006, Eric Wafukho invited me to a religious leaders' meeting in Tseikuru, Mwingi, to help build leadership capacity in the religious institution so it would evolve into the role of a major driver for development in the community. After listening to the presentation and the impact it had on religious leaders in the meeting, Eric challenged me to scale up the conversation and help develop a model that would showcase what a transformed religious institution looked like. Together with others, he helped plan a meeting, where Kenyans, engaged in transformational development, met. The meeting took place at Parklands Sports Club. My confidence started growing that I had stumbled into something that would help transform Africa – and that the time was right to hit the ground.

Aware of the nature of challenges I was up against, I went to Yatta to develop an impact model that I would use to showcase the impact of practical Christianity and its transformative agenda for communities trapped in the cold grip of demonic influences, poverty and despair. I was convinced that Africa's development was wrapped up in her culture, beliefs and attitudes; that unless these were dealt with, development would be shallow. In order to empower the Yatta community, I had to bring on board anthropological considerations that had shaped their thinking and perspectives about life and destiny.

Shifting Gears

Africa's problems amount to much more than the trillions of dollars, pumped into the continent as foreign aid, can solve. It is believed that in the last fifty years, Africa has received several trillion dollars in aid, yet there's little to show for it. These funds have gone into oiling corruption and undertaking facility-based development that has not led to expected human development.

How could a continent blessed with vast resources such as gold, diamond, copper, iron ore, cobalt, oil, natural gas, titanium, uranium, wildlife, rivers, lakes, mountains and forests, and people turn out to be a net recipient of donation from the West? What has gone wrong and what continues to feed the malaise?

The global initiative to identify and focus energy and resources, under the flagship of Millennium Development Goals (MDGs), has demonstrated what is possible when people come together. My experience, working with the poor of Yatta, in Eastern Kenya, has, however, led me to conclude that while global and local initiatives come with the most noble of intentions, the definitions, attitudes and approaches are peripheral and remain oddly minimalist in the face of mounting poverty and despair.

World leaders, stung by the dehumanizing impact of poverty in Africa, have acted in ways they thought would improve the quality of life of a desperate people, but those efforts have fallen flat – because of focus on facility rather than people development. As Dambisa Moyo has observed in her book *Dead Aid,* the billions of dollars that have made their way into Africa have not landed in strategic areas; they have gone into funding the fantasies of the rich while the poor have remained trapped in threatening poverty.

The Millennium Development Goals that have since been replaced by Sustainable Development Goals (SDGs) were the world's time-bound and quantified targets for addressing extreme poverty – in its many dimensions and manifestations – by 2015.

But has that effort faired any better? Has the narrative changed? What we know today is that years down the line, the continent reels in poverty, food insecurity reigns, and health indicators show high child and maternal mortality. Safe water to drink continues to be a mirage, and the gap between the rich and the poor has never grown wider.

Given the intractable nature of poverty and its gory impact on people, the MDGs were designed to be a lasting answer to Africa's woes. Indeed, looking at the laudable goals set in place then, complete with timelines to meet measurable targets, one can't fail but feel the urgency and spirit of the leaders who sought to save Africa.

The table on next page illustrates the development timetable as was envisioned by the brains behind the vision.

MDG	Measurement	1990	2015
1. Eradicate extreme poverty and hunger	%age of population living on less than USD1.25 a day	47%	14%
2. Achieve universal education	Primary school net enrollment rate	52%	80%
3. Promote Gender Equality and Women Empowerment	Number of girls enrolled for every 100 boys enrolled	74	103
4. Reduce Child Mortality	Under-five deaths for every 1,000 births	90	43
5. Improve Maternal Health	%age of births attended by skilled health personnel	59%	71%
6. Combat HIV/AIDS, Malaria and other diseases	Number of infections of HIV/AIDs from 2000 to 2013	3.5 million	2.1 million
7. Ensure Environmental Sustainability	Number of people with access to piped drinking water	2.3bn	4.2bn
8. Develop a Global Partnership for Development	Number of people with cell phones	738 million	7 billion

Extracted from Millennium Development Goals Report

Looking at the table, one doesn't have to be a rocket scientist to understand the extent of failure visionaries of the Millennium Development Goals suffered. No wonder the world felt the need to upgrade to a newer approach, which became known as Sustainable Development Goals. It is the failure of this new approach that has prompted people like me to pull away from the crowd and systematically think things through. The question we are asking is not a new one, but one that is a lot more urgent now: what is the lasting solution? The current scenario, where Africa has been trying to develop by focusing on technology and infrastructure is deficient. It fails to deal with the greatest omission and the most key asset to development: people's worldview and mindset.

So how is worldview and mindset the pivot of Africa's development? How have the twin issues of worldview and mindset been at the heart of failure to crack the hard nut of poverty in Africa? That is the focus of this book.

In the arid Eastern Kenya village of Yatta, in Ukambani, I have worked with the local community to tackle the problem of poverty and restoration of human dignity. The great successes we have witnessed as people have turned what was once an arid land of despair into a green land of hope has not only emerged as a model for communities across the land, but has become a dependable lifeline for the people of Africa who adopt the tenets of the model.

Yatta's Problem was Africa's Problem

The problem of Yatta was Africa's problem. Africa was defined by animism – an arena where ancestors ruled and where poverty was explained as the will of the gods. Animism offered no initiative, no innovation and no hope. The result was a deadly status quo where stagnation of communities became the norm. As was the case in many parts of Africa, my Kamba community was caught up in this web of stagnation and lives were lost in droves.

As a people, we became reliant on relief food (mwolyo) and political contestations became predictably built around the theme of *who would supply food*. That was how votes were earned. Instead of changing our worldview and mindset, we got deeper into the quagmire of failed practices that relied on rain-fed agriculture. We were, thus, left at the mercy of the gods due to erratic nature of rainfall. Our communal mindset had firmly shut our eyes to the realm of new and bold possibilities.

The spirits of the living-dead, the fierce patrons of the underworld, ruled our waters and we would not till the land until those fearsome spirits gave permission, which was often accompanied by great sacrifice.

Spiritism Gave Way to Dependency Syndrome

Dependency syndrome, as was the case in many parts of Africa, became rife in Yatta – and across Kenya. People sank to the level of beggars, kneeling in painful humility for handouts from the government. The thematic *Serikali saidia* or *Please, Government, help us* disenfranchised communities and denied them an opportunity to be the drivers of their own lives and destiny. They did not see any aspect of development in the communities as their own and failed to take ownership, always waiting to be fed, thought for, directed and felt mercy on. In other words, they lived because they were pitied!

To understand the scope of this mindset, let me give the example of a visit to Hola, an arid region in the eastern part of Kenya. While there, I saw a relatively new water pump that had broken down. It had been lying there for a couple of months, yet the community could not fix it in spite of the urgent need for water. They were waiting for the NGO that set it up to come fix it.

I later visited another Eastern Kenya community, where leaders gathered at a training session. When they were asked, at the start of the critical meeting to state their expectations, the leaders, instead of being grateful for the training that had been brought to them free of charge, asked how much their allowance would be for attending the training. It was as if in anything they did, they had to depend on someone else. They even had to get help to do something as mundane as sit and listen.

The Yatta Model

Armed with the conviction that without mindset change development would continue to be a mirage, I searched the scriptures and studied our African reality. I asked myself why cassava, in Ukambani, was eaten raw and not processed into other products. Why was it planted on the ridges and not in a whole *shamba* or farm? And why were cassava cuttings, in Masinga, discarded instead of being used as manure to increase the harvest? Without knowing it, I was coming up with a new worldview – a liberated Christian worldview that was interrogating life from a different perspective. I soon realized how critical this interrogation was and why the religious institutions had to create a platform for this new narrative in the community.

As a result of this introspective process, I designed a Community Transformation Model that has come to be known in Africa as the Yatta Model. It is based on my contextualized interpretation of scriptural teachings on God's creationism and how God purposefully designed His commands on wealth-creation to spark communal prosperity and spur national development.

It is a model that zeroes-in-on mindset change and an empowered worldview as the sure answer to challenges facing Africa. This foundational concept of mindset and worldview shift relocates communities from the realm of slavery and dependency to the realm of empowerment, where they can chart their destiny. It pursues human resource-based development as opposed to the failed project-based development approach.

In the Yatta Model, I make the argument that Western resources should be channeled towards transformation of mindset and worldview among Africans so that adoption of the right technologies and strategies may be at the core of the development agenda. The twenty-first century African should be helped to adopt, improve and appropriate technologies into the development equation rather than given endless prescribed handouts that lack in sustainability in seriousness about eradicating poverty by dealing with its root causes.

The Yatta Model also advocates strengthening of systems and structures that help in midwifing transformational community development. In this regard, seven levels of functional government are identified:

a. The individual level

This is where change starts. Any true change that comes to a community must start with individuals. It is changed individuals that will change their communities through their interconnected levels of influence.

b. Family level

Through a transformed mindset and a shift in worldview, the place of children and women in the family changes as their capacity is built, nurtured and mobilised for the transformation of families and communities. The youth, who normally have a higher capacity for adaptation, are given space and the ability to access the instruments of development. This ensures collective responsibility for growth and ownership of the successes and failures.

Under this Yatta Model, a husband is viewed as President in the home while a wife is viewed as the Prime Minister. This is a deliberate play on the political arrangement that brought President Mwai Kibaki and Opposition leader Raila Odinga into a coalition government, where the two became equals in the affairs of state. The Yatta Model has adopted this arrangement as a contextualized way of pointing out to unsophisticated rural Africans the central role played by the partnership of a husband and wife in the harmonious management of a successful home. Such a home is key to midwifing transformational community development and has to be encouraged.

c. Village level

Villages vary in the number of families located in them and in the geographic region of their placement. They are a critical component that is often forgotten in the equation of development partners. Most development organisations focus on Community Based Organisations (CBOs), which have a set number of villages in their plans and come with specific objectives that are set by the donors themselves. If we were to use these CBOs to advance community interests, we would have to undo the entire framework upon which their model is anchored.

The Yatta Model focuses on converting these CBOs into village structures like agricultural groups. These serve as catalysts in wealth and job creation through production, value-addition and strategic marketing. The focus here is in the deliberate development of people as opposed to development of projects because people will live without projects, but projects will not live without people. Accelerative growth is only achievable where people have embraced transformation in mindset and a radical shift in worldview.

d. Religious institution level

Religious institutions are a critical player in any community. They are among institutions in the community with known and dependable structures, networks and serve as first responders in times of crises. They serve as catalysts for sustained development whenever meaningfully enlisted in the process of development. Community development can't take place without engaging the religious institutions.

e. County or civic government level

The county government, through devolved structures, plays a critical role in ensuring there's a conducive policy regime and that infrastructure and all resources are mobilised to enhance community transformation. They are a leading player in the creation of a peaceful environment – with enhanced security – so that all aspects of development may take place within the enabling environment of calmness.

f. National or central government level

The national government – like its county counterpart – plays a critical role in ensuring there's a conducive policy regime and that infrastructure and all resources are mobilised to enhance community transformation at national level.

g. International or global community level

The international or global community retains the critical role of partnering with all the aforementioned layers of government in order to ensure only the most strategic partnerships are developed.

I have presented these seven levels of government in a summarized format for now – only to whet our appetites. We will delve deeper into them later. It is my goal and hope that this book will spur new thinking and help create a new reality for Africa. May that reality be based on integration of transformed worldviews, synchronised systems and structures, and adaptation of technological innovation for the growth of enterprise and sustainable development. That is my prayer!

INTRODUCTON

INTO THE TRENCHES

Nestled deep in a bend, just off a dusty gravel road that cuts through Yatta, is an expansive demonstrative farm that Christian Impact Mission uses to teach the ten core pillars of mindset change and a shift in worldview. The farm is home to crops, animals, plants and systems that work in coordinated harmony to maximize output while minimizing input. It has been set up to demonstrate that with a transformed mindset – based on ten anchoring principles I have developed as I interacted with people, situations and experiences – people can alter the trajectory of their lives and free themselves to pursue a future of self-determination in all facets of life.

Christian Impact Mission, as I already alluded, was born out of frustration with the docile and unhelpful attitude of religious institutions in Africa. I felt the urgent burden of finding a credible alternative to the *spiritual-food-only* approach, which had left communities across the continent reeling under the weight of biting poverty, low expectations and dependence on handouts from well-wishers.

Under this scenario most people in Yatta, much like in other areas of Africa, came to rely heavily on food and other forms of support from donors and development agencies based in Europe and the United States. The Kikamba word *mwolyo* or help came to define an organizing principle that was built around seeking the most help for the people of Yatta. In politics, as in religious institution circles, the most popular leaders were those who had the ability to attract the most help from donors. Leaders of the religious institutions who marshalled the largest share of *mwolyo* were viewed with awe and went on to be revered.

In my study of the Word of God, I found suffering and human poverty to be antithetical to God's nature and His desire for man to live in happiness. I could not reconcile the intense suffering I witnessed around me with the gracious and loving nature of God.

There was a problem.

It was the desire to figure out what the problem was – and eliminate it for the restoration of man – that led me down the path to discovery of His purpose for man. As I later interacted with key ministers of the Gospel, men ordained by God to reflect the character of the Creator here on earth, I realized that the missing link was not in what was said, but in what was not done. There was a lot more talk about faith, salvation and heaven but no talk about how we lived on earth before the time came for us all to go to heaven. We were on earth but not given the tools to handle being on earth as Christians. I was bothered by a Gospel that left people wallowing in abject poverty, left them trapped in demonic ritualism and reduced them to the indignities of begging to live. The God I had been reading about in the Bible was far kinder, gentler and had greater plans for man than the gory circumstances around me suggested. Feeling the urgent urge to share my thoughts with fellow leaders in the religious institutions, I started talking openly about a gap in what we preached. As this went on, I realized that my burden was the burden of many others.

As the Lord continued to reveal His purpose in my life, I opened my heart and left room wide enough for Him to occupy. It was under these circumstances that Christian Impact Mission was later founded. Starting its missionary work among the rural poor of Yatta, it faced the early distresses of rejection, jeer and suspicion. It fought to rid the community of demonic activities, inexplicable deaths, diseases and deep ignorance. It battled to liberate minds and present an alternative approach to the one cast in the deadly narrative of fear, death and eternal damnation.

The journey that began seven years ago was embraced by members of the Yatta community and has evolved into a thriving example of the power of a transformed mindset and reformed worldview. To be sure we all benefit from the urgent lessons of this book, I intend to use case studies and examples to amplify principles designed to help us on the journey of transformation.

When I finally got down to putting pen to paper on these foundational principles, I received invaluable feedback from great scholars like Pete Ondeng, Professor Kivutha Kibwana and others. Based on their assessment, and my conclusions, what you hold in your hand is a revolutionary discussion that will help communities across Africa get started on the exciting journey to transformation.

Does this book, therefore, prescribe the Yatta Model as the only sure model out there? No at all. I believe there are many development models just as worthy. I, however, invite you to consider this model as the most far-reaching alternative one due to its holistic approach – and based on the anthropological considerations addressed, which are a critical missing element in most others.

Operation Mwolyo Out

To launch us into this vigorous demonstration of the power of transformed minds, we need to meet the deeply focused Chairlady of Operation Mwolyo Out (OMO) in Yatta. OMO is an initiative of Christian Impact Mission and is credited with turning what was once an arid land of poverty and pain into a thriving community of hard work and hope. Jane has this to say:

> Yes, we were old, but when CIM came to us with the challenge for the community to move from depending on erratic *mwolyo* or relief aid to embracing irrigation agriculture, we were the first to take up the challenge,

Into the Trenches—43

even before the religious institutions and the community caught the vision.

We believed we could do it ourselves and through the merry-go-round design, we donated labour and went to each homestead, assisting one another to dig up water pans. Slowly, we moved from digging a few pans to more than three thousand pans in just four years. Today, the number of women involved in the project has grown from the initial forty five to three thousand – of all ages and from all over Yatta Division.

These pans have made it possible for us to plant and harvest sweet potatoes, pumpkins, cassava, water melons, mangoes, paw paws and sunflower, among others. We now have enough food to eat and even extra to sell and earn a decent income. We have also ventured into poultry and cattle farming and are actively exploring newer avenues of creating food security for our community.

The story of Jane – and of these women – is the story of more than five thousand families in the Yatta catchment area, a semi-arid area long considered one of the poorest in Kenya. These families have benefited from the work of Christian Impact Mission by accepting the challenge to transform their mindset by getting out of the *mbokisi* or box mentality; and alter an enslaving worldview. We are, more than ever, committed to building the capacity of communities across Kenya and Africa so that they may drive their own development and take control of their destiny. The pastoralist Pokot community, in northern

Kenya, is the next great frontier Christian Impact Mission has fixed her gaze because people there are in dire need of liberation from forces bent on trapping them in poverty and destructive animistic and militaristic influences.

A Model to the World

After years of designing, implementing and reviewing the Yatta Model, Christian Impact Mission is finally ready to release the development model to the rest of the world as one of the fastest ways of getting out of poverty. This is one of the three modules that we have put together to help build capacity for groups, families, institutions, governments, and religious institutions in order to realise sustainable development.

As we work through the book, we are going to refer to the model as the CIM Model rather than the Yatta Model, in recognition of the inspiring fact that semi-arid Yatta has given birth to a revolutionary development concept that has grown bigger than her. You are about to interact with underlying principles that guide practice of the practical adaptation process CIM is championing in Yatta and in satellite adaptation centres replicating the *transformative* CIM Model in Kenya, Tanzania, Malawi, Rwanda, Ethiopia and elsewhere in Africa.

CHAPTER ONE

UNDERSTANDING DEVELOPMENT

INTRODUCTION

Community development is about people, not projects. It is about moving people from a helpless state of limitation, lack, deprivation and powerlessness to a fulfilling state of empowerment, abundance, wellness, resilience and self-reliance as people take the reins of their destiny.

Based on CIM's experience in Yatta, we know that it is impossible to deliver development without addressing the issues of vision, structures, systems and leadership. Communities must be moved into a place where they embrace an empowering vision – one harnessed through empowering systems and structures by means of a transformative leadership.

Most definitions of community development initially have their focus at the right place – in the community – but later proceed to talk about projects. In the long run, and with the best of intentions, they end up focusing on project development, not community development.

While community development may refer to various interventions designed to move people into a more empowered state – a state in which they drive their own development – the actual transformation takes place in the lives of people and the community. This is referred to as community transformation.

Development is as old as the human race. It started with God himself, when He molded His creation and placed the human race in a stewardship role, commanding Adam and Eve to be fruitful and multiply, and to have dominion over creation. In Yatta, we remain keenly aware that the role we have chosen for ourselves – of empowering the community through transformation of the mind – is CIM's statement about partnering with God to make life better for His children. It is an act of worship!

In recent times, however, most of the players in global development can be traced to post-Second World War, with the creation of such bodies as the United Nations and its affiliates: United Nations Development Programme, and United Nations Children Education Fund.

These bodies were formed on the strength of the desire to bring to an end human suffering and pain, to increase the quality of life of global communities, and to enhance a sense of global citizenship through community building as a people of one race – the human race.

After the Second World War, the world entered the age of the struggle for independence and formation of nation-states in Africa and other parts of the world. As these nation-states came into being, they took greater roles in moving communities within their borders to economic prosperity and structured social progress. Kenya, for example, identified three key challenges that needed to be overcome in order to place her on a path to progress. These were disease, poverty and ignorance.

Around that same time, many humanitarian movements emerged: World Relief, World Vision, Red Cross, Tear Fund, Oxfam (UK), Samaritan's Purse and Compassion International, among others. These agencies committed themselves to the arduous task of addressing the plight of the poor around the world through relief, advocacy and long-term development initiatives. The initiatives were to be undertaken in collaborative partnership with local community structures and government agencies. Many more development agencies have since emerged.

Governments also set up development arms that would support and nurture development efforts around the world and advance their interests. These included OAU, European Union, USAID, DANIDA, AUSAID, SADDC, JICA, ECOWAS, EAC and CARICOM.

To bolster the work of these national and global bodies, research centres and universities have, over the years, made great strides in addressing the plight of the community through research, knowledge generation and provision of various research-related services to the public. In Kenya, groups like Kenya Agricultural Research Institute (KARI) have been critical in doing the above. KARI has provided advisory services, management of the national gene bank, technical back-stopping and capacity building to agricultural sector line ministries. Farmers and other institutions dealing with agricultural research for development have also benefited.

Corporate Social Responsibility

In Kenya, as in other young African nations, the business community saw need to join the community development bandwagon and came up with legalised corporate social responsibility (CSR) to help address community needs in areas such as education, health, and arts. In the recent past, the CSR platform has yielded to a longer and more strategic view of doing business with communities as an empowerment and capacity-building strategy. The faith community has not been left behind. It has been at the forefront of addressing the holistic needs of communities around the world. Work of religious institutions around the world will be treated later; suffice it to say that there has been a growing recognition of the role of the faith community in development matters.

Groups like Tearfund have come up with their UMOJA programme as a tool that seeks to mobilise religious institutions in addressing needs in communities. World Vision has set up a department called Christian Commitments, an entity that seeks to, among other mandates, develop strategic partnerships with religious institutions in promoting human transformation and bearing witness to the good news of the kingdom of God.

Against this backdrop of achievements, the CIM Model seeks to build on the efforts and to contribute to the body of knowledge and its application. In going through this training, one will see various points of convergence with other models and, equally, various points of departure from existing models.

Development

The concept of development, like other Western-inspired ones, has gone through stages of enlightenment as key players have adapted to new realities. In the days of old, development partners acted on the stage of moral and strategic superiority, causing them to adopt ways that have proved more harmful than helpful. The earliest mindset among development partners has today been referred to as the Traditional Worldview Mindset. Its identifying characteristics are listed:

- Development is focused on facility and hardware rather than on people.
- Development is focused on the gaps communities have rather than capacity-building.
- In some cases, development is focused on assets (ABCD).
- The place of God is missing or is weakened in the development agenda, with many donors putting pressure on development agencies not to proselytise.
- Development is packaged in an artificial project mindset, with key elements disjointed from each other. The know-it-all attitude fails to connect with reality and guarantees failure.

- Development is exclusively in the firm hands of development agencies and the government with communities playing the role of passive recipients.

In Yatta, working with lowly peasants meant we had to get to the bottom of the issues that had kept the head of the community under water – causing people to drown in deep poverty. We had to gain the trust of community members by getting to the bottom of the challenges that had caused men to flee Yatta, caused women to resort to brewing illicit beer and witches and sorcerers in the role of deciders of people's fate. We became aware that for the Yatta community to change, there needed to be a mindset transformation so that rather than the reign of powers associated with darkness ruling the day, the reign of powers associated with light would take hold.

The beginning of the end began on the day I walked to a market, where people had gathered to trade and made the stunning announcement that from then henceforth, no one would die again. I warned the witches and black magicians to turn in their paraphernalia of evil because their reign of terror had come to an end. What followed was death of the leading sorcerer, a woman who had given birth to two children – a handsome baby boy and a snake. Her death caused a stir as people began to realize that I was protected by a force greater than the one that had protected the woman.

The Sunday after her death, people came from all over Yatta to listen to the Word of God and they realized that the God of Christianity was more powerful than witches. I was cast in the role of a missionary in an instant, crowned by the weary people of a village to lead them out of poverty, pain and despair. Together with my wife, Reverend Agnes Masika, we preached the Good News of a risen Christ, but we knew that the people of Yatta needed much more than hope could offer – they needed a father-God who took care of their health, gave them good clothes and acted with swiftness to protect them from the fierce forces of evil in the village. They wanted to be free!

Freedom, however, came in the form of trading evil in the village for dependence on relief. It was like giving up the familiarity of African sorcery for the wizardry of *mwolyo* or relief. As Christian Impact Mission, we worked with the community to free ourselves of the new form of slavery that had silently crept in. We made people realize that *mwolyo* appeared harmless and was provided by great people like members of Parliament, relief agencies and religious institutions, but it was unreliable and dehumanizing. It made them beg to live – a gift God gave freely.

Seven years later, the movement we started as Operation Mwolyo Out has caught fire and the people of Yatta are on the way to full liberation. The transformation in mindset and worldview has enabled the community to adopt irrigation agriculture and low-cost agricultural practices that have resulted in availability of food in Yatta all-year-round. In the middle of a scorching sun, a land of dry riverbeds, water pans have made it possible for six thousand families to farm throughout the year and sell their produce in markets as far removed as Nairobi.

Given the successes, Christian Impact Mission has come up with an alternative approach to matters development. We propose that what a development agency needs to meet the needs of Africa's poor more meaningfully is a partnership with local players – those that rely on a model already perfected by the people of Yatta through Christian Impact Mission. Here are the core characteristics of the Transformed Empowered Worldview and Mindset approach to development:

- Development is focused on people, dealing with their anthropological experiences and mindsets and worldviews. It puts people first.
- Development is focused on gaps and goes beyond assets (ABDCD) and focuses on people.
- God is put left, front and centre in development without apology. It is an approach that purposely integrates spirituality in matters of development.
- Development considers people's anthropological experiences. Their beliefs and values are taken into account as core components of development; not just the assets or gaps that they might have.
- Development is not a project but an integrated process in which people are being transformed and are transforming their environment as God's agents of transformation.

The subject of development has been around for quite some time. It has occupied the mind and thoughts of the great and small. It has been the subject of international conversation and been at the front and centre of quest for elective leadership in communities.

The *Business Dictionary* defines development as:

> The process of economic and social transformation that is based on complex cultural and environmental factors and their interactions.

The key terms in this definition are: *the process* and *transformation*. These terms imply that development is a journey and not a destination. It is a journey of change – change that takes place on the economic and social front.

Through this journey of change, poverty is confronted. It is hotly targeted as *a surmountable human condition of deprivation, where people are excluded from the essential relationships that may lead them to fulfill their God-given potential, and where they may suffer unacceptably and have their very survival threatened.*

The fact that poverty is a surmountable human condition and not a permanent one gives hope and lends voice to the urgent human efforts aimed at alleviating poverty through interventions that form the development agenda.

Approach to Development

As we have already established, the definition and approach to development is based on the worldview of whoever is tackling the subject. In studying development, we have identified and clustered two predominant worldviews and mindsets that have shaped universal understanding and practice. There is the

Traditional Worldview and Mindset, and there is what we refer to as the Transformed Empowered Worldview and Mindset.

In our clustering, the Traditional Worldview and Mindset has, within its gamut, all other expressions such as secularism, dualism and animism – replete with its superstitions and fear; and its next of kin, fatalism. It consigns communities to perpetual dependence on aid and on external interventions for their welfare. This fatalistic tendency is more pronounced in some contexts and is what we have come to call in Yatta – where a development model emerged – a *mwolyo* or dependence mindset. It is defeatist in nature.

A Transformed Empowered Worldview and Mindset, on the other hand, is born out of interrogation of the existing worldviews and development and is made up of such worldviews as the Christian or the biblical worldview, the *koinonia* or community well-being, and a hybrid of the Greek and Hebrew worldviews, which have shaped learning and education.

The common denominator in the worldviews, under the banner of the Transformed Empowered Worldview and Mindset, is their refreshingly empowering effect on individuals and the community.

Contrasting Approaches of the Twin Worldviews

It is not enough that the two worldviews be discussed in abstract terms; we need to delve deeply into how they define and shape modern understanding of community development.

a. Facility development vs. human development

Traditional Worldview and Mindset approach views development from a physical plate of that which can be touched, can be felt and can be seen. The focus is on a development philosophy that is hinged on facilities development. It is assumed that if infrastructure and facilities are fully developed, they will lead to human development. This is often not the case. Examples of facility development would include:

- Investing in the development of infrastructure such as rail and transport network as an end in itself.
- Investing in food security that addresses availability without necessarily being accessible or properly utilized by all for nutritional needs.

In the Transformed Empowered Worldview and Mindset approach, development is about developing people. The founding fathers of Kenya and Tanzania had their philosophy of development engraved on human development. This was their worldview. The worldview of the late Julius Nyerere, of Tanzania, can be seen in the following statement:

> For the truth is that development means the development of people. Roads, buildings, the increases of crop output, and other things of this nature, are not development; they are only tools of development. A new road extends a man's freedom only if he travels upon it. An increase in the number of school buildings is development only if those buildings can be, and are

being used to develop the minds and the understanding of people. An increase in the output of wheat, maize or beans, is only development if it leads to the better nutrition of people. An expansion of cotton, coffee, or sisal crop is development only if these things can be sold, and the money used for other things which improve health, comfort, and understanding of the people. Development which is not development of people may be of interest to historians in the year 3000; it is irrelevant to the kind of future which is created (Dr. Julius Nyerere, Freedom and Development, Pg. 59).

The development model we have adopted in Yatta has been built on the foundation that it is people who need to be transformed; that when people are transformed they will transform their environment. To dig even deeper into the nature of the competing approaches, we need to look at key development components through the lenses of the two worldviews:

i. Water sanitation and hygiene (WASH)

In Traditional Worldview and Mindset approach, WASH means making effort to ensure households have access to water in sufficient quantities for domestic, farming and dairy needs – and that they have sufficient sanitation facilities. The table in the next page illustrates global trends in water use by sector.

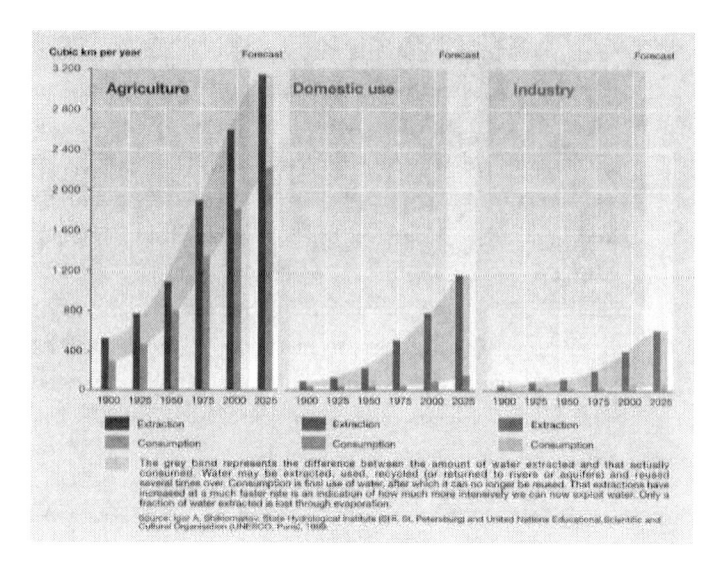

Global Trend water Use by Sector

In the Transformed Empowered Worldview and Mindset approach, WASH not only means making effort to ensure households have access to water in sufficient quantities for domestic, farming and dairy needs; and have sufficient sanitation facilities, but that they are using these facilities with an understanding of the critical role hygiene plays in community health. WASH also means accessing water in a sustainable way, and handling that resource as stewards of the environment.

This component has been critical, especially in the arid and semi-arid areas, and has brought to the table a conversation about the role of water in development.

ii. Education

In Traditional Worldview and Mindset approach, education means the presence of schools, the development of physical infrastructure like classrooms, and availability of teachers and learning material. It is focused on producing graduates intent on seeking white collar jobs but deficient in job creation and innovation. In the last ten years, for example, Kenya has seen a steady rise in enrollment of students in the public and private sector, spread as the following table shows:

Year/Sector	2004	2005	2006	2007	2008	2009	2010
Public	7,394,262	7,597,28	7,632,11	7,330,14	7,508,74	7,693,915	8,300,000
Private	272,355	368,312	371,995	889,122	1,024,05	1,049,170	1,100,000
Total	7,666,617	7,965,59	8,004,10	8,219,27	8,532,80	8,743,085	9,400,000

Source: Republic of Kenya, Ministry of Education- Taskforce Report on Re-alignment of the Education Sector to the Constitution of Kenya 2010, February 2012

In the Transformed Empowered Worldview and Mindset approach, education goes beyond the presence of schools, the development of physical infrastructure like classrooms; and availability of teachers and learning materials. It focuses on access and quality of education and its capacity to equip a young nation to handle its unfolding challenges ahead.

Learning outcomes such as skills in numeracy, literacy and oracy – balanced with emotional intelligence and other general life skills and attitudes – are needed to drive society forward and build nationhood and global citizenship.

iii. Health and nutrition

In Traditional Worldview and Mindset approach, health and nutrition focuses on establishment of health facilities, including such edifices as laboratories, theatres, maternity wards, palliative care centres, and nurseries; and ensuring these facilities are well-staffed and well-equipped with machines and drugs.

In Transformed Empowered Worldview and *Mindset* approach, health and nutrition does not just mean establishment of health facilities like laboratories, theatres, maternity wards, palliative care centres and nurseries – and ensuring these facilities are well-staffed and well-equipped with machines and drugs – but the quality, affordability and access of the healthcare system and its ability to enhance child survival in the face of many challenges obtaining in the context.

Countries like Kenya are doing a lot to ensure health facilities are available at the grassroots level and that there is a sufficient number of health personnel to attend to people.

iv. Food security

In Traditional Worldview and Mindset approach, food security means placing focus on availability, access and utilization. In many contexts, there is perpetual preoccupation with relief food, which often creates a spirit of dependence. The *Mwolyo Syndrome*, as captured in the worldview that obtained in Yatta, is a case in point.

In Transformed Empowered Worldview and *Mindset* approach, land is seen as a resource that is to be developed through an agricultural value-chain that would create food security and nourish the needs of the earth in a sustainable way. Food security is not just focused on availability, access and utilization, but on stability factors that deal with production and supply as well.

On the matter of food security, even the writer of the book of Ecclesiastes has a comment to make:

> Moreover the profit of the earth is for all: the king himself is served by the field (Ecc. 5:9, KJV).

Indeed, as we have done in Yatta, emphasis in the TEWM approach is placed on industrial agriculture that leads to sustainability.

b. Gaps vs. potential in the community

In Traditional Worldview and Mindset approach, development efforts focus on addressing gaps in the community. This, inadvertently, shifts communities into a *lack* or *dependency* mindset. The pro-poor organisations have a great deal of effort to make in ensuring that by focusing on the poor, they do not place communities in a retrogressive mode – a mode in which communities and individuals begin to compete amongst themselves to see who is poorer so as to gain from promised interventions. Focusing on gaps – while it has its place in the efficient deployment of resources – denies communities a chance to accelerate their growth by looking at what they have.

In Transformed Empowered Worldview and *Mindset* approach, focus is placed not on problems and challenges that individuals and households are facing but on the opportunities that are presented in such contexts. Instead of seeing unemployment as a problem, we see unemployed individuals as available labour that could be deployed. It is the *what do you have in your hand* conversation. As communities engage in it, they begin to be solution-builders of their own destiny.

c. Asset based community development vs. human capital in the community

In Traditional Worldview and Mindset approach, Asset Based Community Development is a noble idea that shifts from focusing on gaps in communities to focusing on identifying, mobilising and building on local capacities and resources to transform communities. This is done in a relationship and networked manner, with an external agent – but is directed by the internal process of self-discovery.

Our experience, in semi-arid Yatta, has made us realize that God endowed every community with resources that need to be tapped, not only for the current generation but for subsequent generations as well. However, the focus, in this worldview, is on what people have in a material sense rather than the sum total of what they bring to the table even in their lowly state. It fails to take into account what and who people are.

In Transformed Empowered Worldview and *Mindset* approach, there is recognition of people as being the greatest asset. Their mindset and worldview is thus viewed as the greatest impediment to or the greatest facilitator of community development. Consequently, it starts a conversation that focuses on people and what they are becoming. It recognises that transformed people will transform their society.

d. Secular vs. spirituality and place of god in development

In Traditional Worldview and Mindset approach, propelled by an increasingly secular donor community, secularism has gained currency in development circles, with deliberate efforts made to ensure resources do not go into addressing spiritual needs in communities. In the secular mindset, human challenges are assumed to reside in the physical realm and solutions are assumed to reside there too. A belief of this nature, however, can only be entertained until spiritual forces pitch camp in a school and keep children away from class; or until a calamity of global proportions, like a tsunami, hits a nation and caused devastation beyond the capacity of man to cope with on a physical level.

Interestingly, while some in the donor community would want no attention paid to spirituality, they are quick to impose values and conditions on aid, most of which are repugnant to the recipient community's sensibilities. This has been true in Africa in relation to the institution of marriage and forms of governance. Even organisations with strong Christian roots have found themselves between a rock and a hard place in terms of fulfilling their mandate and mission on the one hand, and honoring stringent donor conditions, on the other.

Tearfund, Compassion and World Vision are among those that factor spirituality in their development programmes.

While not discounting the place of spirituality, the second component of this worldview is dualism. Dualism has been influenced by popular thought that confines the functions and realm of religion to the spiritual and leaves matters of the flesh and the physical world, and order of life, to human agents and governments of the world. Even traditional humanitarian development agencies, many born out of an integrated approach to life, have, over the years, succumbed to dualism in the West and have often failed to strategically engage religious institutions in Africa. They have ignored other religious groups in the community as well, working with most of them only on the periphery of community mobilisation.

It is worth noting that Western civilizations benefited immensely from products of Christian movements like the Puritans and Quakers, who moved to the newfound lands and established schools like Harvard, Yale and Princeton. Others helped to establish strong economies, founded on rooted biblical principles. For the West to turn around and deny Africa this foundational spiritual ingredient of transformation when they are beneficiaries is to take hypocrisy and ignorance of the facts at play to the highest level. It was through the strong spirituality of William Wilberforce and the Quakers that slave trade was finally abolished, business networks developed, banking initiatives set up and politics transformed. Indeed religious institutions brought education, education brought science and philosophy, which later brought technology;

technology brought modernism, and modernism brought civilization; civilization has now led to post-modernism.

In the words of Prof. Mbiti, *Africans are notoriously religious*. To deny Africans the liberating power of the Christian worldview and mindset, and abandon them to an animistic one, steeped in witchcraft and superstition, is to abandon a people at their most vulnerable of times.

When Agnes and I first came to Yatta, our neighbours, steeped in animism, attributed crop failure to ancestral spirits that were unhappy. They had to offer sacrifices for crops to do well. Based on our Christian worldview, which taught dominion through innovation, change and adaptation to climate change, we introduced to the Yatta residents the concept of harvested water and developed adaptation strategies that yielded a bumper harvest.

It was that bumper harvest that started to change minds and made us realize that no amount of capacity-building, in five-star hotels, could deal with entrenched animism. There had to be a spiritual dimension to address it.

Landa, writing with deep anguish, goes to great lengths to explain how Evangelical thought has embraced dualism to the detriment of development in the last 150 years. He says:

> But as evangelicals we talk about salvation message, being born again, born again believers, born again churches, the new birth, Jesus saves, as though the initial experience of salvation is the only message. Jesus

> preached that the only way to enter the kingdom of heaven is through Himself; but He constantly put salvation in the context of the broader message of the kingdom of heaven. He never referred to the gospel of salvation. Jesus taught the gospel of the Kingdom: salvation and the truth about every dimension of life. Yet, more than 150 years of mission work has been dominated by this concept of salvation as our singular goal. The result of this truncated message is no less tragic than a grown child still incapable of doing anything for himself. Something has gone terribly wrong. God's design has been interrupted, and this life has not fully developed (Landa Cope, An Introduction to the Old Testament Template – Rediscovering God's Principles for Discipling all Nations, Pg. 20-21).

In Transformed Empowered Worldview and *Mindset* approach, the spiritual dimension is a critical component of development in which God is discerned to be at work as the giver and sustainer of life. In this mindset, development seeks to engage God in a working partnership that affects the way of life of communities and nations and not just material affluence.

Recognizing that there are spiritual forces that seek to deny nations and communities access to abundant life, including socio-economic and political transformation, this mindset engages in spiritual warfare with such tools as prayer, scripture search, fellowship, faith in God and a message of peace and justice. Development, in the African context, is viewed through the prism of religious beliefs too. Any transformation that overlooks this obvious phenomenon is bound to amount to nothing.

American social and political transformation was driven by Rev. Martin Luther King, who heavily appealed to the American religious consciousness. Apartheid, in South Africa, was fundamentally a religious mistake. Bishop Desmond Tutu appealed to the religious consciousness of the nation while working within the narrow framework of existing political avenues. In much the same manner, Africa's colonisers depended heavily on the Christian missionaries to pacify Africans for their penetration. It was to God the African was willing to stand down!

Indeed, Christian ethics are proven sinews in community cohesiveness. No community that forsakes God on the fleeting platform of material affluence will stand. What this means is this: all actors in the development agenda, including the donor community, will need to tread with caution and guard against separating matters of faith and those of development. Development agencies will have to guard against seeking development without values, and material affluence without character – because it will be like building a house on quicksand. Aware of the weight of this matter, the Lord issued a warning to a young nation – a warning all nations will do well to heed (Deuteronomy 8:8-20):

> A land of wheat, and barley, and vines, and fig trees, and pomegranates; a land of oil olive, and honey;

⁹ A land wherein thou shalt eat bread without scarceness, thou shalt not lack any thing in it; a land whose stones are iron, and out of whose hills thou mayest dig brass.

¹⁰ When thou hast eaten and art full, then thou shalt bless the LORD thy God for the good land which he hath given thee.

¹¹ Beware that thou forget not the LORD thy God, in not keeping his commandments, and his judgments, and his statutes, which I command thee this day:

¹² Lest when thou hast eaten and art full, and hast built goodly houses, and dwelt therein;

¹³ And when thy herds and thy flocks multiply, and thy silver and thy gold is multiplied, and all that thou hast is multiplied;

¹⁴ Then thine heart be lifted up, and thou forget the LORD thy God, which brought thee forth out of the land of Egypt, from the house of bondage;

¹⁵ Who led thee through that great and terrible wilderness, wherein were fiery serpents, and scorpions, and drought, where there was no water; who brought thee forth water out of the rock of flint;

¹⁶ Who fed thee in the wilderness with manna, which thy fathers knew not, that he might humble thee, and that he might prove thee, to do thee good at thy latter end;

¹⁷ And thou say in thine heart, My power and the might of mine hand hath gotten me this wealth.

[18] But thou shalt remember the LORD thy God: for <u>it is he that giveth thee power to get wealth,</u> that he may establish his covenant which he swear unto thy fathers, as it is this day.

[19] And it shall be, if thou do at all forget the LORD thy God, and walk after other gods, and serve them, and worship them, I testify against you this day that ye shall surely perish.

[20] As the nations which the LORD destroyeth before your face, so shall ye perish; because ye would not be obedient unto the voice of the LORD your God (KJV).

e. Project mindset vs. livelihoods

In Traditional Worldview and Mindset approach, the project mindset views community life as disjointed and carries out interventions in one area without benefiting from the interconnectedness of community life. It seeks to address education without realizing that the school-going child needs food in order to stay in school and be healthy. It seeks to provide such facilities as sanitary pads to school girls without addressing their other needs – often leading to resale of such pads to address those other pressing needs.

In Transformed Empowered Worldview and *Mindset* approach, community life is perceived in totality and interventions are handled at the livelihoods level. This is, perhaps, the latest shift in development conversation. This approach seeks to integrate all the interventions and focus on the wellbeing of households, realizing that intervention in one area does not necessarily improve the quality of life of households unless other areas are also covered in an integrated manner. It is an approach that is user-friendly to community engagement as members of the community know life must be addressed holistically.

Consider the following figures that highlight rainfall patterns and different livelihood clusters in Kenya. There is a strong correlation between rainfall patterns in the country and the livelihood clusters. The clusters demonstrate a high reliance on rain-fed agriculture.

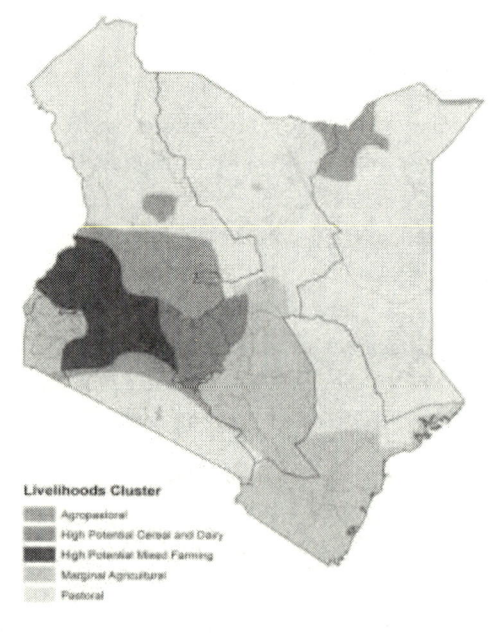

Livelihoods Cluster
Source: Famine Early Warning System (FEWS) Network

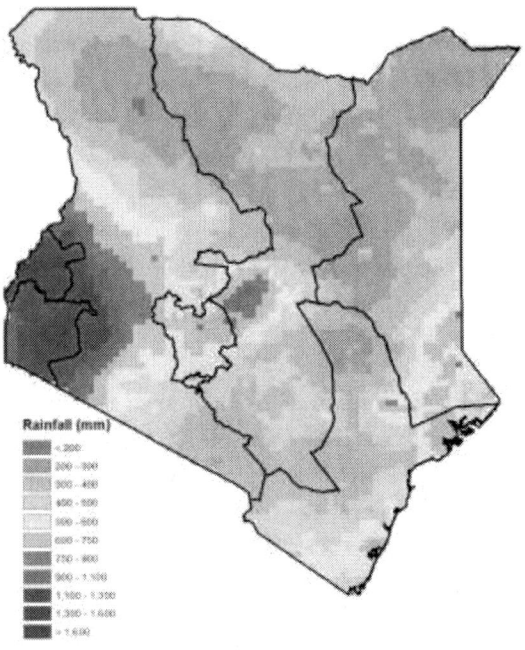

Average Annual Total rainfall
Source: Famine Early Warning System (FEWS) Network

f. People owned processes vs. external actors

In Traditional Worldview and Mindset approach, communities sit on their laurels as external agents set the agenda and content of development. It is this failure to demand local action and direction by donor agencies that is, perhaps, the greatest disservice ever done to Africa. It can be seen in the manner **Call for Proposals** is designed – done in ways that portray fixedness in strategy and high specificity on the personnel and means of delivery.

The African continent has been a recipient of aid for the last four decades. Non-Governmental Organizations have poured millions of dollars into Africa, and yet African communities still remain poor (Moyo 2008). Moyo makes this unyielding statement out of frustration – aware that nothing short of shift in donor mindset will work for Africa. Development agencies that continue to feed Africa on the *mwolyo* or help approach have to be helped to understand that there is a better approach today; an approach that restores dignity.

In Transformed Empowered Worldview and *Mindset* approach, communities give leadership to their own development and progress. Mzee Jomo Kenyatta, in Kenya, at independence, challenged Kenyans not to sleep on their laurels but to get to work and address the key challenges facing the nation. Here are the words that sounded like a war cry:

> Many people may think that, now there is 'uhuru' (freedom), now I can see the sun of Freedom shinning, richness will pour down like manna from Heaven. I tell you there will be nothing from Heaven. We must all work hard, with our hands, to save ourselves from poverty, ignorance, and disease.

Guided by a worldview that saw development as being about people, Kenyatta galvanized his resolve in the Harambee spirit of pulling together to address the challenges that faced Kenya. He gave the nation a work ethic and a focus that would place the nation on a growth trajectory.

Based on our assessment of struggles of the past – the minimal results showcased by development agencies after years of engagement and deployment of vast resources – we have been forced to conclude that African communities need new approaches to community transformation. The lessons learnt in Yatta are at the heart of this assertion. We bring to the table a new approach, where African communities need to be engaged in the transformation of their communities. We also propose that African communities be helped to help themselves; that they need to explore resources and opportunities in their backyards before they invite external aid.

At inception of the Yatta Transformation Programme, the community developed a ten-point exit strategic plan. It was designed to free us from dependence on aid. Those ten points, as they have led to great successes across Yatta, have evolved into pillars. They include:

- Community Mobilisation
- One-Acre Rule Miracle
- Gender in Development
- Integration in Development
- Market Linkage
- Value Addition and Village Commercialization
- Investment
- Environmental Concerns
- Agri-nutrition
- Advocacy

The Yatta worldview holds that while development may be catalyzed by many actors, it is best driven by those in the context in which the legitimate interests of various actors are integrated on the value-chain. It is propelled by those whose interest it is to mobilise and build on the internal capacities, structures and indigenous knowledge of the community.

In this worldview, development has a viral effect that once started in a corner, spreads to other spheres. We hold that the starting point of this transformative process is and must be the individual, then the family, then community, then a nation, and finally the world. In essence, therefore, development under this worldview is a stewardship responsibility. Stewardship is the mantle which operates all progressive causes – human rights, conservation, economic welfare, government reform and oversight, education, healthcare, disaster relief, animal welfare, mental health, and peace.

As God changes and transforms a people, they will change and transform their environment. This is the lesson of Yatta, the miracle we have witnessed as mindsets are changed and people have adopted a new worldview – Operation Mwolyo Out!

The Jesus Approach

The founding fathers of Kenya and Tanzania espoused a philosophy of investing in human capital. This was the very same philosophy Jesus gave the world on transformation. It was hinged on transformation of the individual to ultimately transform the community. This individual-community nexus was critical for the form of transformation in which an individual influenced the community and the community, in turn, influenced the individual.

While the focus on infrastructure and facilities by many African governments and other development agents has a place, such efforts may not bear much fruit unless a drastic shift is made to move to people-based transformation. This is what will bring faster development and guarantee sustainability.

No More Theory, Practical Solutions Now

Much has been written on the state of affairs in Africa. There has been a rising chorus that what Africa needs is not aid but business partnerships. Some have even argued that the aid that comes to Africa is the reason behind the continent's sorry state of affairs. It is hard to dispute the findings of these authors if you have never been in the trenches. In this book, however, I put forth a compelling new approach to matters of community development – based on the popular Yatta Model. This model, which has transformed mindsets and turned the fortunes of the semi-arid lands of an eastern Kenya village around, has made us realize our responsibility, as our brother's keeper, to share the secrets. We feel obligated to give the world the recipe, the coded formula that has the ability to end poverty everywhere. As Christian Impact Mission (CIM), we bring the Yatta Model to the global stage for consideration on the urgent matter of community development.

In *DEAD AID, WHY AID IS NOT WORKING AND HOW THERE IS ANOTHER WAY FOR AFRICA,* Dambisa Moyo reviews her worldview as she takes a journey of reflection to help shed light on the negative impact of aid on the continent. She argues that aid could reduce savings and investment, be inflationary and choke off the export sector, among other vices. She says there must be another way and proceeds to explore what this other way would look like, including trade, capital solution and banking the unbanked.

As our contribution to this on-going conversation, the CIM Model presents what could, perhaps, be the solution Africa has been looking for. In the chapters that follow, you will be urgently confronted – not with an intellectual treatise – but with evidence of transformation, with Yatta being the first case of how a systematic thought and execution of programmes is changing a community that had been considered one of the poorest; with unproductive land. Because Yatta is today food-secure, actively engaged in wealth-creation, with evidence of improved livelihoods, we've been sent on a mission.

The CIM Model, as we shall see, does provide a new paradigm of engagement in which African governments and the donor community find space to engage in new and transformational ways. What it does is bring to the table a uniqueness that has been missing in many other development models.

- First, that development starts with transformation of people's worldview as the hardware of development; and that any other approach is too expensive and not sustainable at all.
- Second, that meaningful development is driven neither by a government nor a donor agency, but by the people

themselves, with the government and donor agencies playing a supportive role. There is need for reversal in approaches so that the story of transformation may be told by communities rather than the current scenario, where communities are a mere supporting cast on the canvass of global engagement.

- Third, that the solution to Africa's development might not be in further research and studies, but adaptation through systematic thought processes and execution.

Reflection

a. What is your perspective on the myriad traditional development models that focus on community gaps and target the vulnerable in the community with aid projects?

b. The CIM development model does not reject other models, but seeks to say that in ADDITION to these initiatives, deliberate effort needs to be harnessed in the goal of value-addition. Going through contrasts in the chapter on worldviews, what new insights do you need to bring on board in your context?

c. Dambisa Moyo, in her book *Dead Aid* has argued that the architecture of foreign aid (not humanitarian or emergency aid) to Africa has been part of the problem and has not translated to stronger economies and better leadership. Why, in your opinion, do African nations find it easier to look for this kind of aid instead of exploiting local resources?

CHAPTER TWO

CHANGE IN MINDSET

The place was an arid land. The vegetation Agnes and I saw when we arrived was dry grass, cactus and thorns. The heat was overpowering and relentless, occasionally slowed down by intense thunderstorms that left gapping galleys in their wake. We were in Yatta to embark on one of the most important assignments of our life. We came armed with the conviction that God created us with the ability to fill the earth and subdue it – that Christians had the moral obligation to lead the way in transforming the world and making it a better place.

We had the will, but where were we to start? In a place like the Yatta of then, danger lurked in each corner one looked. Because of the dry riverbeds and dusty water pans, venomous tropical snakes and other terrifying reptiles slithered into homes and pitched camp around pots and pans. There, they lay in wait, daring anyone to act in hostility. Indeed, it was because of the dryness of the land that the eastern lands of Kenya became known as the most dangerous where it concerned snakes. They bit people in the morning, at midday and even at night – killing those who could not be rushed to the ill-equipped hospitals that dotted the landscape.

If it wasn't the snakes, it was the animals. In a land where there was hardly any leaves for domesticated animals to eat, cows, goats and sheep died in droves in the dry seasons. Aware of this phenomenon, wild animals like the spotted hyena, leopards and guerillas roamed the land, some sitting right next to the emaciated dying animal, marking time as it awaited the death of the cow or sheep or goat.

The night, however, was the most terrifying time of all. It was the hour night runners, black magicians and witches went around casting their spell in the village. Woe unto anyone who was unlucky to meet any of these evil players. And again, the night was the time some of the most dangerous wild cats and largest snakes came out of their hiding places. Some of them were said to have been owned by the sorcerers, who used them to kill, extort and demand respect in the community.

More than once, I asked myself whether Agnes and I were doing the right thing camping in the hostile territory, a land we could feel was controlled by the ferocious forces of darkness. We could tell that Yatta, like much of Africa, was a land firmly in the grip of demonic forces, who had erected altars in each corner. The land was under a curse, defiled by evil and left to the deadly designs of the forces of demonic ritualism. Nothing could prosper in Yatta, we feared, as long as the worship of Satan – he who comes to steal, kill and destroy – was the only form of worship that took place in Yatta.

Yatta was crying for redemption!

We arrived quietly, intent on making our *hostile* debut in the community a low-key affair – to avoid exposing ourselves to early attack. We knew that those we found in the area were not going to suddenly welcome strangers and treat us as cherished guests. In any case, I had come to the land with a daughter of the Luo, a tribe that lived along Lake Victoria and was reviled as the *Bavirondo* – a derogatory reference.

As a Christian minister, I watched the devastating activities of evil with consternation and wondered whether we would ever manage to turn the Yatta community around. The impact of evil was grave. The level of anger, hunger and despair was high and palpable. The donors who had been in the region had all but given up, fearing that nothing good would ever come out of a place where stinging poverty, ignorance and satanic rituals conspired to harvest the souls of men.

Surprisingly, it didn't take too long for the war on satanic activity to be won – what took long was the war on *transforming* the mind of the Yatta people. It took a while for us to gain the trust of the people and take tentative steps to introduce the concept of water pans and irrigation agriculture. Indeed, at first it was only women who responded – and this coming at a time Agnes was still in Nairobi to meet the requirements of her contract. I was alone with the women of Yatta, something for which I was viewed with suspicion, skepticism and hostility.

After Agnes joined me, her first order of business was to seek the men of Yatta in what she dubbed Operation Men Back.

The community's men had gone to other towns in search of a better life – most never to return. With time, many of them were located and persuaded to come back home to their wives. Some came back broken, cut down by the merciless hug of HIV-AIDS. Others were willing to stay and take a measure of the glories promised by the man with a Luo wife, but took to drinking in the meantime – to drown their sorrows.

If anyone wanted to understand the impact of sin on man, which made God send Christ to die for us, it was on display in Yatta. Yatta was the epicenter of satanic zeal, a place demonic agents used as the laboratory where new evils were invented to torment God's people and frustrate the plan of salvation.

With determination, we got families in Yatta to engage in an ingenious African approach known as merry-go-round. With donated labour, women dug water pans deep enough to withstand the impact of the sweltering sun. Those baby steps led to bigger steps as we all embarked on more grandiose ideas. The power of God's hand was made manifest when, within a year, the first crops planted yielded a bumper harvest and those with initial reservations and resistance to irrigation farming joined the bandwagon.

Not long after, I started sensing something. I felt that the size of the harvest we experienced – on a rolling basis – was more than enough to sustain life in the village. We could stop depending on *mwolyo* or food aid to live. We could become free! But more than anything, I sensed that God was finally giving me the formula to restore the dignity of His children in a land once held captive by evil. The curse of satanic influence was about to be destroyed!

Christian Impact Ministry, at this point, felt the need to make the Yatta Model a vehicle for the redemption of God's people. We drew the community into a unity of purpose, where our goals metamorphosed from merely having abundance in food to adopting the liberating philosophy that championed dignity and self-reliance rather than dependence on relief aid. As the philosophy caught fire and spread to neighbouring villages, we felt bold enough to radicalise its edges, sharpening its tenets into a battle cry we dubbed Operation Mwolyo Out or OMO.

Today, the transformative impact of OMO has galvanized a community and a region. More than six thousand families have dug water pans deep enough to rely on just one massive downpour a year. There are water pans that have been sunk to depths as low as twenty four feet down. Because of the water pans, farmers in the Yatta community no longer rely on rain-fed agriculture; they farm all-year-round. Many of them have adopted practices like value-addition and value-chain agriculture, where a product like maize or corn is not just roasted or boiled, but the husks, stalks and cobs are used to meet another need. This ensures the least possible wastage and maximum use of farming space.

Margaret's Testimony

In an earlier chapter, we heard from Jane, the chairperson of OMO. In this chapter, we need to hear from the treasurer of OMO's horticultural wing. Her name is Margaret Kameti.

Since childhood, I had always known *mwolyo* or relief as the mainstay in my village. We dutifully queued for *mwolyo* throughout my childhood, right into adulthood. Even after I got married, we still queued for *mwolyo* to feed our families.

I was, however, never comfortable about reliance on *mwolyo* and felt it was wrong. In 2009, when CIM came up with a mobilisation programme, in which they were mobilising and teaching communities to be self-reliant, my husband and I attended the meetings and decided enough was enough. *Mwolyo's* time was over. We began to dig a water pan in our compound.

Unfortunately, even after we got our own water pan, we continued queuing for *mwolyo* and did not realise our full breakthrough until we had dealt with the spiritual matters in our lives.

Today my family grows almost everything on our three-acre farm, supported by a large water pan that holds water even during long spells of drought. We grow chilies, tomatoes, sweet potatoes, French beans and even grafted mangoes. It is a miracle. Most of our produce is sold at wholesale prices in the market.

We also sell to Everest Export Company and to a number of middlemen who now frequent our area. It is a dream come true for us and we thank the Almighty God for everything.

Like the story of Jane, this inspiring story of Margaret and her family is the story of more than six thousand families in the Yatta catchment area. These families are benefiting from the work of Christian Impact Mission (CIM) and have seen their lives transformed from a life of perpetual begging to one of empowerment. They have powerfully demonstrated how a shift in mindset can have an impact on development. Through their example CIM has been able to reach communities farther afield and we are in the process of moving into East Pokot with the same transformational community development philosophy we have put to excellent use in our Yatta backyard.

Mindset

We have said a lot about mindset. You would have expected that by now a rigorous definition of the word would have shown up somewhere in the discussion, but we had to save it for this moment. According to one dictionary, a mindset is:

> A fixed mental attitude or disposition that *predetermines* a person's responses to and interpretations of situations, an inclination or a habit (italicized emphasis mine).

Our mindset is like cement; once it is set, it is difficult to change. Development initiatives that do not address mindset are doomed to be superficial at best and to leave no lasting impact at worst. It is not impossible, but it is very difficult to deliver real development without addressing the issue of mindset. It is like giving people a brave new world to live in without giving them a manual to live by. Whatever attitudes and dispositions they inherited in the old world will be ushered into the new world as a point of reference. This is why we say meaningful development can only take place within the context of a transformed mindset – a changed worldview.

In Yatta, I have worked with the community to reconfigure the mindset of its people. Operation Mwolyo Out has acted as an anchor upon which farmers have built structures and systems with the ability to free them from dependence on relief aid. The community has taken the reigns of its destiny in its hands. There is no *Serikali saidia* or *Government, please help us* mentality anymore. For us to have an even deeper understanding of the impact of mindset, we need to interrogate the symbiotic nature of mindset and development in a transformed community.

Symbiosis of Mindset and Development

In the last couple of years, we have received several visitors in Yatta. Christian Impact Mission has hosted professors from universities in Kenya, leaders from World Vision, partners from religious institutions within and outside Kenya, and political leaders like members of Parliament, members of County Assemblies, and governors. Their coming has caused farmers in Yatta to ask some of the basic questions most lowly communities ask when transformation begins to take place. In this segment, I want us to consider some of these questions so that we may better understand why mindset and development must go hand in hand for there to be sustainability. The first question has to do with identity.

   a. **Who are we and what resources do we have?** If you had asked the people of Yatta that question eight years ago, they would have looked you in the eye and said,

> "We have nothing. We are a poor people only kept alive by *mwolyo*."

They would have been right.

Today farmers in Yatta have embraced irrigation agriculture and many of them have become wealthy. They have left the days of poverty and despair behind, going about life with the dignity of proud pioneers of transformation in a once defeated community. The point is – what a community believes about itself is a significant factor in addressing development.

In Traditional Worldview and Mindset approach, individuals and communities have *a grasshopper mindset* in which they view themselves as weak, vulnerable; and as victims of circumstances. They exhibit *Serikali saidia* or *Government help us* mindset that seeks help on a perpetual basis. This mindset about identity is further reinforced by development actors who portray people as weak, poor, disadvantaged and vulnerable. It is, indeed, interesting that *poverty definitions* are often imposed on the community by external development actors. This is what Margaret, the treasurer of OMO's horticultural wing, described about her family's situation before transformation.

In Transformed Empowered Worldview and *Mindset* approach, individuals and communities have an exalted and realistic view of themselves and are reluctant to allow circumstances that they are under to define them. This requires a mindset change that appeals to people's identity in God and their destiny in this life. If you were to meet Margaret today, you would agree with me that her mind has completely been transformed. She no longer allows adversity or setbacks to define her because she has relocated her spiritual roots to Calvary and allowed herself the dignity of becoming a key player in the shaping of her destiny.

A transformed worldview is an empowering force that respects the "soul competency" that God has made people with capacity to think and to drive their own destinies. This mindset invites a development worker to join a development story that the communities and individuals are writing on the canvass of time and eternity. Elsewhere, it is called respect!

b. Whose responsibility is it to drive the development agenda?

In the Traditional Worldview and Mindset approach, the community believes it is helpless and all help must come from elsewhere – from the government and other development actors. The result is a community that is forever dependent and vulnerable. It is a *mwolyo* community, a sad community where people refuse to think outside the *mbokisi* or box.

As was the case in Yatta, before CIM came in, application of donor aid in Africa has sometimes led to a state where community initiatives have been left crippled. This has been partly due to the manner in which aid was given. It created a dependency syndrome, which was a stronghold that kept most of Africa poor. It began with government extension officers who came into communities with ready prepared packages for adoption and passed those on as a reason to love and respect political leaders affiliated to the government.

This harsh phenomenon of waiting for things to be done by someone else is sometimes perpetuated through the presence of external actors, who own and manipulate the means of production, decision-making and marketing. Even community structures such as CBOs are formed not for transformation but in readiness to receive aid. They can hardly be referred to as community structures as their identity, structure and operations are heavily donor-defined and donor-dependent. Sadly, there is a tendency by the NGO world to go around individuals and the community of faith and target CBOs, many of which are a creation of a *mwolyo* mindset and were formed solely as conduits for freebies.

The situation is exacerbated by the absence of strong advocacy programmes, focused on policy-influence and mindset-change. Cheap political campaigns in Africa that promise *utopia* without calculating an accompanying work ethic have produced dependent and vulnerable nations and communities that wait for solutions from London, Paris, Zurich, Copenhagen, Oslo, Washington, Bonn, Tokyo, Beijing, Moscow and Amsterdam.

African leaders are busy visiting Western nations, begging these nations for funds to help develop Africa, yet they have failed to borrow technology and mobilise collective resolve in Africa to harness Africa's resources – including human resources, agricultural potential, vast minerals, oil and geothermal energy. The net result is perpetuation of successive generations of dependency. Indeed, most CBOs and NGOs are busy writing proposals for continuous capacity-building without ever addressing that for which the capacity is built.

As we learned earlier in the book, development of the Western world has been greatly influenced by religious institutions. These institutions have been the custodian of development. The history of development and civilization in the West is tied to religious institutions as light and salt. The institutions have enhanced value-based development that respect processes of growth. This serves as the cure and best fight against corruption, which seeks to short-circuit and circumnavigate the natural process of wealth-creation and power-management.

CIM has, over the passage of time, offered the moral code of the community in Yatta. It retains the capacity to offer greater inspiration and act as a catalyst for transformation.

In Transformed Empowered Worldview and *Mindset* approach, the community believes it has resources and the will to drive its own development agenda; and it is actively looking for partnership spaces that facilitate its development. The government and other development actors are seen as catalysts and aid is channeled into community priorities and critical areas that build the community's capacity to drive its own agenda and support others.

In this mindset, the responsibility to drive development starts with the individual – the skills and attitudes that need changing. It then goes to the family as a primary player in the community; then to religious institutions as custodians of values and vehicles of community-change. It finally goes to groups and community structures like CBOs and Civil Government.

Kenya's Vision 2030 seeks to build this reality in which there is a just and cohesive society that enjoys equitable social development in a clean and secure environment. We have made a strong start in Yatta, through CIM; we hope other communities will follow our example and replicate the CIM Model in every part of Africa – so that human dignity, which a *mwolyo* mindset ripped from us, may be restored.

c. What is the role of aid in community development?

In the Traditional Worldview and Mindset approach, aid is given in perpetuity, often as its own end. In Yatta, for example, donor agencies were prepared to give aid and then give some more, never planning a weaning process. This results in creating heavily dependent communities and vulnerable households – which is what happened with Margaret's family. The challenge often encountered is the strict conditionalities attached to aid. They virtually render the aid ineffective in its choice of priorities. It feels like a trap.

The largest culprit in the aid priorities has been lack of focus in building community capacity to drive their own development agenda. Furthermore, the NGO environment has often not been held accountable to Return on Investment (ROI) by the donor community and regulatory bodies that monitor the cost of doing business. My observation in Yatta is this – if donor agencies put in the barest effort to seek accountability, better results would be seen in people's lives. Without imputing any motive, I have to say it makes one wonder about the sincerity of the efforts. Are they designed to help or to enslave?

Three reasons explain this anomaly: failure by the International Non-governmental Organisation (INGOs) to engage grassroots structures, the high cost of doing business by the INGOs, with huge budget portions going towards offsetting their cost of doing business, and failure to engage an approach that takes into account the anthropological circumstances of the people to be helped. Some INGOs spend 60 dollars for every 100 dollars purely on internal costs and only deliver 40 dollars to the community. Is it any wonder that the highly elaborate, irrelevant and inappropriate strategies have, therefore, caused more pain than solved problems?

The challenge has been exacerbated by the low engagement with grassroots structures and reluctance to have incarnational encounters with the community, with many donors and NGOs forever holding conferences and workshops in five-star hotels – away from communities. There would have been greater impact if such meetings were removed from these hotels and held in the field, where people live. Granted that there is a place for holding training and consultations in such facilities, but care is needed to ensure that we adapt transformational and incarnational models that cater for relevance and effectiveness.

Most development practitioners from the government and NGOs plan in their offices and conclude on what they want to do before they even approach the communities they purport to want to work with. An effective way of conducting training is doing it where the people are as opposed to taking them to five-star hotels, where they are yanked from the familiar and thrown into a world they don't belong to. In such a setting, only a sense of further alienation can be achieved.

Each time I look back at how we began, the brokenness of the people of Yatta in those early days, I am tempted to think that development agencies which bring broken, hurting people like Jane and Margaret to five-star hotels just want to put up a show. These donors come to the villages, take community leaders to big hotels, where they purport to discuss issues, then spell out solutions that were already concluded elsewhere. It feels like a subtle effort in bribery. The action of removing community members from their environment into hotels disorients them, leaving them disillusioned and confused to a point where they lose focus and the planning of the projects in most cases begins on a wrong footing.

And then again, given the nature of fallen man, this action of uprooting leaders from their environment often makes the community suspicious of their leaders. They are regarded as sellouts who may have been given goodies to bring to the community but chose to *eat alone*. Thus the projects, once they get underway, end up being *owned* by the few, losing the felt needs of the community they are working for.

The method of planning also perpetuates dependency, where communities expect the government to plan and deliver to them. It is important that planning for projects be done within the environment where the projects will be delivered. This should be done with the participation of the communities for ownership to develop; otherwise all efforts made afterwards to make the community own these projects are doomed to fail.

This dependency is made worse by a political culture that takes responsibility from citizens by promising to do that which citizens are to do for themselves. The end result is a political environment that replaces the donor, but still disempowers the people. It is like replacing a tiger with a hyena in a kraal!

In the Transformed Empowered Worldview and *Mindset* approach, aid is directed towards building capacity for communities to drive their own development. Such capacity-building includes interventions like facilitating the acquisition of skills, appropriate technologies and equipment, and farm inputs and market linkages.

At CIM, we have noted that a greater sense of accountability makes a tactical shift over time from aid to capital that is repayable and that seeks to build business and entrepreneurial capacity. It is not enough that the families in Yatta be given aid; they have to be equipped to engage in irrigation agriculture on a commercial scale so that empowerment is placed at the core of their path back to full restoration.

The expertise and experience of the NGOs and other Public Benefits Organisations should be mixed with local knowledge and capacities to address development issues faster. Indeed, the government and NGOs should facilitate, guide and give the technical roadmap that is lacking in rural areas, but leave the communities to take charge of their own destiny so that they can own the successes and results of their projects.

Today there is recognition that NGOs or the government can provide all the services that people need, and therefore people should be facilitated to work and generate wealth *themselves* in order for sustainability to be achieved. They should be helped to identify appropriate technology that is adaptable in different areas and let people use this technology to forge their own destiny. In our experience, in Yatta, living in these villages, and aligning whatever challenge to local technologies, is the most effective way of leaving impact on the ground.

The CIM Development Model

The work CIM had done in Yatta has demonstrated the power of transformed mindset. Today, when one talks to pioneers of the CIM Development Plan like Jane and Margaret – and even other families in the greater Yatta catchment area – it will be hard to meet anyone who has not witnessed the remarkable growth the community has experienced. Because of greater involvement in irrigation agriculture and use of locally-available technologies, infant mortality rates, biting poverty and rolling hopelessness have been made a thing of the past.

Operation Mwolyo Out has caused a change in mindset and liberated people to the realm of a new worldview, where fear, demonic activities and laziness rendered them hopeless to a worldview where destiny is shaped by people in Yatta. I always get fired up when I take a walk in the community and see people act innovatively by using available objects like trees, the ground and discarded metallic objects to maximize output in their farms. They have sensed the power of thinking outside the box – they call it getting out of the *mbokisi* mentality.

Aware, of course, of the African's desire to see, not just be told, we have created a model farm on the CIM grounds, in Yatta. The demonstration farm is home to animals, crops and ideas on how to apply local technologies for maximum output. We have worked to lay to rest the myth that planting must take place within the scope of rainy seasons and that when the rains are delayed, it is because the gods are displeased and a sacrifice has to be offered. We have disabused the community of the notion that digging water pans could invite a curse because the deeper ground is home to ancestors and they don't like to be disturbed. We have trashed the belief that agriculture is a rain-fed activity rather than a survival mechanism, where man must plant all-year-round to remain healthy, wealthy and wise.

In the seven years we have been at it, the CIM Development Model has matured into a robust blueprint that relies on key pillars. Here they are in order of priority:

a. Exposure

Taking deliberate steps to expose individuals and a community to new models of reality ignites in them a sense of desire for change. They reason that if someone else could do it, so could they. This is especially powerful when such exposure comes from a context similar to theirs. It explains why a programme that started with limited numbers of people has blossomed into a Yatta-wide, six thousand-family activity.

Exposure demolishes human strongholds that resist change in the name of the uniqueness of their context. The CIM Centre, in Yatta, which we have set up as a demonstration farm, is one such attempt to provide opportunities for many communities to come and experience transformation.

b. Training or gaining knowledge

The mind is willing to make adjustment when it is confronted with facts and truth in convenient portions and served in humility. At the CIM Centre, we have provided an avenue for the Yatta community and visitors to undergo training in a relaxed and non-threatening environment. Through these intense trainings, we have seen the lives of many – like Jane and Margaret – transformed.

In the recent months, the CIM Centre has hosted leaders from as far north as East Pokot and as far out as Tanzania, where a team from World Vision-Tanzania visited for a week. We have taken the model to Bondo, in Siaya County, and visited several other counties to demonstrate the ability of the model to change minds and change lives. We see the demonstration farm as a key tool in exposing people to the possibilities available in development when minds are transformed.

c. Crisis

Sometimes the only option available to embracing a mindset change is when we run out of options through a crisis. This is not what one wishes but sometimes it is the only way. This is especially critical in weaning communities and nations from donor-aid. Through such actions, people are forced to look internally for solutions. Without sounding like CIM wishes crises on any community, I have to say that we've become adept at viewing all manner of crises as learning opportunities that must be exploited to move people from old, unhelpful mindsets. In their low moments, people are more open to interrogating their circumstances and are more inclined to accept newer approaches they would readily reject were storms not threatening.

Inside the CIM Development Model

The Yatta Transformation Programme emerged out of a desire by the community to rid itself of relief aid. As life got better for families in the region – and confidence levels arose about sustainability of the miracle – the community developed a ten point exit strategic plan:

- Mobilisation
- Water-harvesting
- Use of appropriate agricultural technology
- Growing of high-value crops
- Value-addition
- Developing cooperative culture
- Market linkage
- Environmental concerns
- Agri-nutrition
- Advocacy

This exit strategic plan is Christian Impact Mission's most impactful arsenal in the war on poverty and hopelessness. It is a holistic, integrated community transformation programme that has been in place in Yatta since 2006. Our strategy has revolved around *nursing* religious institutions' revitalization process that entails empowering them in the community. We've also worked with existing CBOs and FBOs to become better agents of community development, using participatory approaches throughout all the phases of the programme. These phases, for desired results to be achieved, have been identified as:

- Assessment
- Designating
- Implementation
- Monitoring
- Evaluation
- Reflection
- Transition

Emphasis, in the CIM Development Model or programme, is laid on identification of community priorities, gaps, resources, potential, external and internal barriers, *experiences*, knowledge, and *indigenous technologies*.

On the basis of our successes, and our desire to restore dignity in communities around Africa, CIM has embraced the greater mission of mentoring communities in other parts of the country. Our goal is to promote community identity, creativity, participation and ownership all over Africa.

Reflection

a. Why is it critical to interrogate our understanding of community development before we engage in it?

b. In many parts of the world, development seems to focus on projects and facilities rather than in exploring people's *anthropological* experiences, values, and beliefs. How is this manifest in your community, nation or institution?
c. If worldview and mindset are that critical in pursuing community development, what do we need to do in order to address them?
d. What do we learn from the Yatta experience that may help us in transforming our worldview and mindset?

CHAPTER THREE

WORLDVIEW – RELIGION AND DEVELOPMENT

I recall the day I first mentioned to my parents my intention to marry a beautiful girl from the lake region. Because of my exposure and education, being that I worked in Nairobi, they didn't tell me off – or even attempt to dissuade me – but I could tell the idea was not welcomed. The two had grown up in a land, where a Mkamba married a Mkamba and a Luo married a Luo. Intermarriages were scolded upon and were seen as rebellion that would attract the wrath of the gods. By bringing Agnes home, I was making the statement, according to them, that I was prepared to face down the gods for the sake of love. I was daring the ancestors!

The land was replete with stories of men and women who had attempted to defy the gods and were struck by lightning, died of mysterious illnesses or went mad. There were many stories and songs weaved around the theme of punishment for defiance of the gods, the ancestors or culture. These forms of communication mediums instilled in people the sense that they had to live within the confines of a certain worldview. They had to live within the closed borders of a mindset that limited them to behavior approved by the gods.

When Agnes eventually came home, after we got married, she faced the initial hostility of those who feared she was disaster waiting to happen. From my parents to elders to women in the community, I could tell people were waiting to see the size of punishment the gods would bring down on me – and the day the punishment would be meted. Was it going to be immediate or would it take long? Was it going to be in the form of death or was I going to run mad? And just what would happen to the lady from the lake, the one who had dared defy the gods of the Wakamba? Was she, too, going to be punished?

That rocky start in our marriage eventually gave way to one of the most important relationships in my life. It didn't take long for Agnes to prove her worth in our home. In the first family gathering, a matter arose that needed to be deliberated on. In that moment, Agnes provided ideas that carried the day. The family welcomed her wisdom and Dad ruled that henceforth she needed to be invited at those gatherings. The derogatory term *Bavirondo*, which had been used in describing her Luo community, gradually died down as she earned the respect and admiration of other family members.

By her kindness and inclusivity, Agnes proceeded to change the worldview of those who dreaded the wrath of the gods on account of intermarriage. She made the community realize that the Luo were just as loving and wise as the Akamba. Today my family is a mini United Nations in the Yatta area. I am married to a Luo, my eldest daughter is married to a Luo, my son is married to a Kikuyu lady; and my younger daughter is married to an Igbo, a wonderful man from Nigeria.

Through my family, the people of Yatta have experienced a worldview change and many openly point to us as evidence that the gods have no problem with intermarriage. Indeed, I am of the opinion that as the trend of intermarriage catches fire all over Kenya, we are about to witness one of the most remarkable transformations in Kenyan history – the birth of a *tribeless* society. Its coming has already been heralded by the number of Kenyans married to foreigners abroad, the number of Kenyans married to a spouse from a different tribe, and the ease with which parents marry off children to suitors from outside the framework of an old worldview. Because of the importance of worldview in development, we need to look at this matter in-depth.

What is Worldview?

Worldview is the way of looking at life, its meaning, values and belief systems – that informs how the community behaves. In this discussion, four key worldviews will be critical: Hebrew, Greek, African and Christian. Each of these worldviews has had an impact on any person or community that has come into contact with them – and there is a sense in which they have influenced and shaped each other.

The Christian worldview has been influenced by the Hebrew and Greek worldviews, as can be traced in both the New and the Old Testament. These biblical testaments were written within the context of these worldviews. While both testaments carry one coherent message – which points to God's plan for the human race, through Christ and His work – it is evident, in world history, that the twin worldviews have shaped the world greatly. Their unintended consequences have played a powerful role in unifying global thought around the concept of good versus evil – where good is of heaven and Christ while evil is of hell and Satan.

The Greek Worldview

The Greek worldview focuses on the acquisition of knowledge, philosophy, principles, theories and postulates through analysis and synthesis. It has shaped much of education. It has had a tendency to focus on the mere acquisition of knowledge and not moved into integrating and turning such knowledge into concrete actions. As a result, those who have embraced this worldview have often been good theorists, who have, however, lacked the impetus and drive to identify and undertake actions aimed at delivering communities from the shackles of poverty. This worldview has, however, been good at *monitoring* progress and ensuring *accountable* environments.

The Hebrew Worldview

The Hebrew worldview, on the other hand, has been focused on the application of knowledge. It has been focused on that which is practical, that which gives strategic advantage and moves a community forward through deliberate actions and choices. It has been impatient with mere theories which do not translate into action. In essence, therefore, this worldview has been the business side of knowledge.

Even in its experience of God, this worldview has interacted with God through His actions – as captured in the Hebrew names of God. Here are some of them, in the table below:

Hebrew Name	English
Jehovah Jireh	God as Provider
Jehovah Shalom	God of Peace and harmony
Jehovah Rohi	God the Shepherd
Jehovah Tsidkenu	God the Righteousness
Jehovah Makadesh	God who Sanctifies
Jehovah Rapha	God the Healer
Jehovah Nissi	God the Banner of victory
Jehovah Shammah	God the Present one
Jehovah Sabaoth	God of war and security
Jehovah Yeshua	God who carries Salvation
Jehovah Cheleq	God who Portions
Jehovah Beryth	God who keeps Covenant

The Names of God

I don't know what names the people of Yatta would give God after His powerful manifestations in their lives, but I am sure they would all be names of merited glory. Like in Yatta, I know that the twin worldviews, under discussion, have percolated into African thought and influenced local perceptions. There are many places where the broader African view of life mirrors rather closely the core views of the Greek, the Hebrew and the Christian perspective. In the segment below, I want us to focus on the question of how these *age-old* worldviews have impacted Africa. Is Africa better because of them or are we worse off?

Greek Worldview in African Institutions

The Greek worldview has infiltrated Africa's education system. There is characteristic rigour as evidenced in seminars, theories, institutions, philosophies, papers and viewpoints. This can also be seen in the way many development agencies have placed a high premium on scholarship – even in the most mundane of tasks, like having to have a Masters-level education to be in charge of a project implemented by semiliterate community members in the villages of Africa!

The heavy emphasis on scholarship and academic rigor – not matched by equal emphasis on application by many of these development actors – may have significantly contributed to Africa's stagnation despite the presence of many international development agencies, for the past fifty years.

Hebrew Worldview in African Institutions

On the other hand, the Hebrew worldview has been detested in certain quarters, where pragmatism and action have been the drivers. Here, there has been low tolerance for *endless* meetings and conferences and seminars that the Greek worldview offers.

Sometimes this worldview has failed to benefit from the Greek worldview – which would require such best practices as record-keeping, documentation, researching, mainstreaming and interrogation. *Best practice* ensures that both practice and theory are aligned.

What is the Christian Worldview?

The Christian worldview has been greatly influenced by the two worldviews above, thus just a few points on the Christian worldview will suffice:

a. Christian worldview and environment

God is the *author* of the environment. The Christian worldview brings in the stewardship of God's resources to the fore. This form of stewardship seeks to harness and exploit resources in a sustainable manner – and also in a manner that cares for the environment and God's overall creation. As Chuck Van Engen says:

> Christians care for creation not because it is "mother earth" (New Age paganism), nor because its care guarantees the survival of the human race (secular humanism), but rather because it is the creation of, and is cared for and supported by our heavenly Father in Jesus Christ (Psalm 8, John 1, Col 1, and Eph. 1). We know that there is a link between the salvation of humans and the salvation of the earth. For "the creation waits in eager expectation for the [children] of God to be revealed...in hope that the creation itself will be liberated from its bondage to decay and brought into the glorious freedom of the children of God" (Rom 8:19-22). And we know that the status of creation is intimately connected with the relationship of

humans with God. When humans rebelled against God in the Garden of Eden, creation itself fell. And now "we know that the whole creation has been groaning as in the pains of childbirth right up to the present time… (because) the creation waits in eager expectation for the (children) of God to be revealed" (Rom. 8:22, 19).

b. Christian worldview and technology

Technological advancement is as a result of God's revelation and insights on how to efficiently develop resources. It is about providing efficient ways of production – which *essentially* means to increase productivity. Disassociate God from this and you have glorified science and man. God has been involved in the development of man. Distancing Him from technology is to say that He (God) should not be involved in the development of mankind. This, in itself, is erroneous.

c. Christian worldview and family

The family is a unit that God looks unto. In the Law of Moses and in the New Testament, God instructed man to teach his children to trust God. The family is the pillar of sustained religion in the community. God gives each family space and sees them as a government, where a man is the head and a woman is the prime mover of *family development*. A harmonious working of the husband and wife results in sound development of the children. Deuteronomy 4:9 (KJV) buttresses this point:

> Only take heed to thyself, and keep thy soul   diligently, lest thou forget the things which thine eyes have

seen, and lest they depart from thy heart all the days of thy life: but teach them thy sons, and thy sons' sons.

A Christian Worldview of the Individual

When Jesus came to the world, He did not come for Jerusalem, Jericho or Capernaum, He came to seek and save the lost in Jerusalem, Jericho, Capernaum, and elsewhere. He came for the individual… the thematic *whosoever bears this witness*. It is these individuals that are transformed and reach to others.

Many agencies focus on communities and set up community based organization. While this approach does promise fairness in treatment, it fails to take advantage of how community could be transformed if individuals are targeted. This is one of the pillars that we shall later – in the Transformation Model we have advanced as CIM – speak about forcefully.

The Challenge of Dualism

In Yatta, one of the key challenges we faced was to present all of life as a gift of God. We had to instill the sense that from the rising of the sun, until its going down – in all activities under the sun – the Lord was in it and was to be glorified. Because of that approach, we faced challenges when religious institutions preached the gospel of good versus evil. Inadvertently, this message of good versus evil reinforced the sense that indeed the world was a playing field of the two antagonistic forces. To get a sense of how damaging this was, let us discuss the impact of creating these dichotomies.

The Impact of Creating Dichotomies of Secular and Sacred

The dilemma we faced – and is faced by many today – was the tendency by well-meaning people to divide life into the sacred and the secular. In this context, secular refers to that which denies the place of God in the social dimensions of life. Spirituality is restricted to the songbook and mere reading of the Bible and any other instrument of worship. Those who hold this view believe the world and the sacred ought to be separate. Even the journey of Christian faith has had these challenges, as Chuck Van Engen says:

> A century ago Christian missions generally shared a consensus around a classical view of mission that did not split evangelism and social action. Missiologists generally saw the Gospel as impacting all of life. They had a common definition of mission, articulated and popularized by the watchword of the Student Volunteer Movement (SVM): "The evangelization of the world in this generation."
>
> That "watchword" was later used by John R. Mott as the title of his most famous book and was also adopted as the motto of the great World Missionary Conference of Edinburgh, 1910. The SVM's watchword assumed a somewhat holistic view of mission, even though we must recognize that such a view was too often encased in a Euro-centric goal of Christianization and civilization. Yet even that goal assumed a conversion component. ….The emphasis on social service of a hundred years ago in terms of agriculture, medicine and

education were not seen as activities over-against verbal proclamation and personal faith conversion.

They were seen as integral aspects of proclamation of a Gospel that called for conversion. After the Second World War this changed in North American thinking about mission and a great gulf was created between those who advocated socio-economic and political change over those who affirmed verbal proclamation as being central to mission (Chuck Van Engen, Towards Missiology of Transformation).

This dualism has been perpetuated by certain renderings of scriptures and songs:

Romans 12:2

And be not conformed to this world: but be ye transformed by the renewing of your mind, that ye may prove what is that good, and acceptable, and perfect, will of God (KJV).

Some have reduced this great passage that calls for holy living here on earth – with an eternal perspective through a renewed mind – to a call to decamp to *heavenly concerns* in another world. Another scripture that has been wrongly applied is:

2 Corinthians 6:14-18

Be ye not *unequally* yoked together with unbelievers: for what fellowship hath *righteousness* with unrighteousness? and what communion hath light with darkness?

> [15] And what concord hath Christ with Belial? or what part hath he that believeth with an infidel?
> [16] And what agreement hath the temple of God with idols? for ye are the temple of the living God; as God hath said, I will dwell in them, and walk in them; and I will be their God, and they shall be my people.
> [17] Wherefore come out from among them, and be ye separate, saith the Lord, and touch not the unclean thing; and I will receive you.
> [18] And will be a Father unto you, and ye shall be my sons and daughters, saith the Lord Almighty (KJV; italicized emphasis mine).

This dualism is also reflected in songs. When I was growing up, I used to hear songs like:

> This world is not my home I am just passing by. I have nothing to do with the material things of this world, because my treasure and pleasure is in heaven.

Such songs reinforced the mindset that the material and the spiritual were distinct and separate and could not be pursued simultaneously. This was the same mindset that affected us in Yatta as we got down to the business of transforming lives. As you may well imagine, such dichotomising came with unseen consequences that reverberate to date.

Consequences of these Choices
As a result of this dichotomy, religious institutions have been weak in their full mission and have abandoned this key arena of

life to secular forces. It has been rendered *irrelevant* in many respects, resulting in decay of the society's moral fabric.

This school of thought – where religious institutions have been largely confined to the sacred – seems to be a scheme of the devil to make them irrelevant and have them dismissed in the world market so that secularism takes over. The big question, therefore, is: can real development take place without *integrating spirituality* in the total way of life of a people?

Africa is at a stage where it is reassessing donor engagement, given conditionalities attached to much of donor aid – most of which touch on human rights. The problem is that *human rights* is a blanket to put donor values on the table, some of which are repugnant to Africa's definition of morality.

A development programme that doesn't engage the culture of the community is doomed to fail at its core mandate. We must engage the way people perceive reality, pursue their destiny and practice their beliefs and priorities if we are to succeed.

Challenge of Animism

The challenge of Africa is not just dualism – which is often a burden given to Africa by development agencies and *modernity*; her real challenge is animism.

A development worker, who comes into a community and designs a WASH – Water Sanitation and Hygiene programme – that seeks to address hygiene issues by helping to provide latrines in the village, may discover that there may be low usage of the facility due to cultural values and beliefs held by the community concerning the use of a latrine. This is what affected us at CIM, when we faced resistance to dig water pans because of fear that our ancestors would be disturbed.

Equally, any education programme that seeks to highlight the importance of education to the youth by showcasing successful members of the larger society may soon discover that such members, while commanding global fame, may not be held as role models in the community. Instead, role models may be the illiterate members who control large herds of cattle in the village and are considered warriors.

But the greater dangers of animism, perhaps, have to do with accepting a fatalistic view of the challenges in which people find themselves – the view that these challenges are caused by enemies, arising out of jealousy. Consequently, everybody tries hard not to look successful in society so as to avoid the *kukunikilwa na ndunduli* or *being looked at with a bad eye*.

So then, if worldview is that *critical* to the development agenda of a people, how does one *influence* it to facilitate development? How does one integrate the Hebrew and Greek worldviews above? How does one get to change lenses and begin to see the spiritual and physical as two sides of the same coin of reality?

a. When a crisis hits

Our thinking and our value system will be shaken and shaped by reality as it unfolds. Such reality check will invite us to reassess our assumptions, our values and our priorities.

In medicine, the positive correlation between men not being circumcised and the spread of HIV and AIDS has caused many cultures to embrace circumcision of their men, a practice that had hitherto been alien. The impact visited by the HIV and AIDS on communities – including reversing gains in such areas as child survival programmes, household incomes, food security and education access, among others – has called for concerted efforts to identify cultural and other practices that could be exacerbating the situation.

Through engagement of historical community structures, and sustained conversation with cultural gatekeepers, communities have had to rethink some of their practices in times of peril. We shall see later, in the Yatta example, how a crisis brought about a reassessment of the cultural beliefs and practices.

b. When revelation is obtained

After returning from exile, Israelites came up with new laws about work. They made it impossible to do any work on the Sabbath. History shows that her neighbours, aware of this fact, attacked her on Sabbath. However, the coming of Jesus Christ and His healing ministry – in which He healed on Sabbath – caused Israel to revisit her theology and fight for survival on Sabbaths too. Christ revealed the acceptability of shifting thought to align with the challenges of the moment. By extension, what He revealed was that God expected man to use his creative power to have dominion over the circumstances around him. He made us the masters of our destiny.

c. Through the regeneration work of the Holy Spirit

This is spelt out in the book of 1st Corinthians 2:12-15 (KJV):

> Now we have received, not the spirit of the world, but the spirit which is of God; that we might know the things that are freely given to us of God.
>
> [13] Which things also we speak, not in the words which man's wisdom teacheth, but which the Holy Ghost teacheth; comparing spiritual things with spiritual.
>
> [14] But the natural man receiveth not the things of the Spirit of God: for they are foolishness unto him: neither can he know them, because they are spiritually discerned.
>
> [15] But he that is spiritual judgeth all things, yet he himself is judged of no man.
>
> [16] For who hath known the mind of the Lord, that he may instruct him? but we have the mind of Christ.

Knowledge is gained either through revelation or through research. When it is acquired, it changes the way business is conducted. In a sense, therefore, a society that stops thinking stops growing and begins to die. Unfortunately, many African villages are net exporters of human capital in which their sons and daughters, who have received quality education, migrate to the capital cities of the world without ever returning to plough back their knowledge and experiences and improve the lives of their community. They remain abroad, only writing papers and dissertations about their countries, but never fully engaging the core issues of the continent.

Indeed, the sad reality is that many African professionals return to the village only when they are dead – to be buried. Farming is left in the hands of their *ageing* parents, without ever benefiting from the expertise for which the world pays them handsomely as consultants. This is the very essence of witchcraft!

The situation is made worse by a political mobilisation culture that is often not concerned about the plight of the people, but is focused on how to capitalize on such plight to catapult or maintain itself in leadership.

This Calls for Real Leadership

Changing worldviews is a leadership function. It calls for a leadership that is willing to confront the challenges of its time and help move communities into *new stages* of progress. Society and institutions are organised around leadership. When such leadership is committed to working with all stakeholders to address the needs, and position constituents for *transformation*, the product is progress. Whenever leadership is focused on self-preservation, however, decay and strife reigns.

Harry S. Truman, a former American President, says:

> Men make history and not the other way around. In periods where there is no leadership, society stands still. Progress occurs when courageous, skillful leaders seize the opportunity to change things for the better.

Servant leadership is what Agnes and I offered the people of Yatta at a time the land felt cursed. At the risk of communal rejection and failure, we trusted God to use us in the long journey to transform semi-arid Yatta. We borrowed ideas from Professor Willy Addei, who came up with three Rs about responsive leadership to culture and values. He said:

- **Retain** - those positive values and practices that should be retained and mainstreamed in corporate behavior.
- **Reject** - those values and practices that no longer serve the good of the community and that are repugnant to social development and progress.
- **Reform** - those values and practices that need to be modified and adjusted in order to serve the shared interests of a community better.

The great journey we began in Yatta is not one that will end in our time – it carries on into the future. On the basis of God's call to uplift His people, we came to a land overridden with sorcery and decay – starting with nothing but our pension money – and led a community to *reconnect* with God's purpose for its sons and daughters. We have given the people of Yatta a new dimension in life – the dimension of a biblical worldview, the ability to continually assess new threats and answer them by thinking outside the box of past or current cultural trends. If that is what leaving a legacy is all about, Agnes and I have done our bit and await a crown of glory in heaven. And if we had it to start the journey all over again, we wouldn't change a thing because nothing has ever been more exhilarating than walking in faith – only trusting that God will make it happen!

Reflection

a. Reflect on this scripture, Deuteronomy 3:10-20 (KJV):

When thou hast eaten and art full, then thou shalt bless the LORD thy God for the good land which he hath given thee.

¹¹ Beware that thou forget not the LORD thy God, in not keeping his commandments, and his judgments, and his statutes, which I command thee this day:

¹² Lest when thou hast eaten and art full, and hast built goodly houses, and dwelt therein;

¹³ And when thy herds and thy flocks multiply, and thy silver and thy gold is multiplied, and all that thou hast is multiplied;

¹⁴ Then thine heart be lifted up, and thou forget the LORD thy God, which brought thee forth out of the land of Egypt, from the house of bondage;

¹⁵ Who led thee through that great and terrible wilderness, wherein were fiery serpents, and scorpions, and drought, where there was no water; who brought thee forth water out of the rock of flint;

¹⁶ Who fed thee in the wilderness with manna, which thy fathers knew not, that he might humble thee, and that he might prove thee, to do thee good at thy latter end;

¹⁷ And thou say in thine heart, My power and the might of mine hand hath gotten me this wealth.

¹⁸ But thou shalt remember the LORD thy God: for it is he that giveth thee power to get wealth, that he may

establish his covenant which he sware unto thy fathers, as it is this day.

¹⁹ And it shall be, if thou do at all forget the LORD thy God, and walk after other gods, and serve them, and worship them, I testify against you this day that ye shall surely perish.

²⁰ As the nations which the LORD destroyeth before your face, so shall ye perish; because ye would not be obedient unto the voice of the LORD your God.

b. Take time and reflect on your own journey. To what extent has your views on development been influenced by upbringing and external influences?
c. In your view, what is the contribution of spirituality to development?

4 CHAPTER FOUR

MOBILISATION PHILOSOPHY

In the Garden of Gethsemane, on that night of deep anguish, Jesus looked up into the heavens and asked God to take away the bitter cup of sorrow from Him. In the days following our arrival in Yatta, I secretly wondered about the wisdom of coming to a place like it at a time I should have been enjoying my retirement. I had worked in some of Kenya's trendiest schools, mingled with the nation's top politicians, educational leaders and doctors, and even adopted the approach of counseling them rather than their children when I concluded that a child's maladjustment at school was a product of dysfunction at home. In my twilight years, what I wanted was to slow down and rest, but there was a force driving me to my own Gethsemane. It was nudging me, leading me to a destiny I could no longer turn my back on.

If you ask me why I chose Yatta as the place for mission, I will tell you it could have been nothing but God's doing. Once there, however, we ran into a firestorm of demonic activity on a scale that we could have never imagined possible. It was like the Lord had answered our prayer for mission by dropping us right into the middle of a haunted graveyard – with terrifying howling winds, shadowy figures with masked faces and fingers with sharpened, long nails. We had been sent on a mission to tame the wildest land and wrestle it from demonic agents. Our task was similar to what Christ's mission on earth had been.

As we got down to business, it didn't take long to assess the mission for what it was – it was a call to mobilise a people and use their feebleness as the greatest weapon against the forces of darkness that had held them captive for so long. Together with Agnes, we rolled back our sleeves and went to war, initially unaware of the scale of the spiritual warfare that had to be wedged to reclaim Yatta. We didn't know that to take back the devastated community, we would have to confront Satan on his turf and use prayer and faith as the only shield against forces bent on destroying us. We could feel the anger, the gritted teeth of evil – the demons wanted us decapitated and our blood fed to their insatiable appetite of doom, but God was going to deliver us from the powers of darkness. It was in Him alone that the power to defeat evil lay.

Not too long after we arrived, our neighbor, a lady, gave birth to twins. She had neither water nor food. In spite of our efforts to keep her safe, her situation of lack worsened and she later died. As I look back, I see that needless death as the turning point in our transformation work in Yatta. We were so moved by the plight of mothers and little children that we could no longer treat the situation as anything other than an emergency. We suddenly got into the mode of fighting an escalated war, determined to usher in a new reign by mobilising people around the need for transformation. As the war began, our eyes were opened to the existence of special altars in the community called *mathembo*. Before each planting season, sacrifices were offered to ancestors at these altars – and they were many, all located in the watering sources. The demonic world was aware that water was the source of livelihood and were eager to use that scarce resource to control the fortunes of the community. The farming cycle, from land preparation to harvesting, and overall water management and economic activity in the community, was dictated by spiritual forces controlled by sorcerers and magicians.

The altars were at:

Katutuni.

Kasooni.

Muliluni.

Musingini.

And Ivutini.

In essence, land, the only available avenue to life, was protected by spirits who would be invoked during sacrifices. During such sacrificial occasions, the *kilumi dance*, a traditional dance using *kithembe* or drums – and lasting one week – was staged in uniform and was designed to invoke the attention of the gods. The dance was coordinated by *ordained*, traditional women priests in the entire region. If a sacrifice was not offered, no tilling, planting, harvesting or eating of farm produce would take place, even if it had rained.

The community was at the mercy of *athiani* or diviners, who instructed the priests, in the *mathembos*, what to do. It depended on their availability and timing, not on rainfall. Failure to offer sacrifices would attract penalty from the ancestors. Drought, crop failure and other calamities were seen as punishment from the gods. This was the prevailing mindset, reinforced by a cold worldview of fear and despair – that we had to mobilise the community against. We had to raise an army of transformed men and women who would take back Yatta from forces that drank the blood of their children at infancy and killed mothers as they gave birth. It had to be an all-out war, based on the book of Deuteronomy 8:18 (KJV):

> But thou shalt remember the LORD thy God: for it is he that giveth thee power to get wealth, that he may establish his covenant which he sware unto thy fathers, as it is this day

Standoff at the Katutuni Shrine

One day – in a scene reminiscent of what happened between Elijah and the priests of Baal – there was a power encounter in which a religious entity mobilised the community to trust God for rain without having to offer a sacrifice to the ancestors on the *mathembos* or altars. A new water pan had been constructed and needed to be filled with water.

While the elders and priests of the *mathembos* mobilised their followers for sacrificial offering, the religious entity mobilised her forces for *faith* in God. It was a war of nerves. Was God going to send the rains and declare victory over *mathembos* or would the rains fail and give the ancestors victory? In that hour of vindication, the Lord sent the waters of heaven and the water pan filled to the brim. Through this, and many other miracles, the community started a slow march to God.

Reverend Steve Mwangangi – the resident pastor in Yatta – narrates how his congregation has grown from a membership of one hundred to more than three thousand, in five branches; with a regular financial contribution more than ten times before the community knew God. The same growth has been noticed in the other denominations in the area.

So ... what is Mobilisation?

As the word suggests, mobilisation has to do with channeling a target group's energy and focus towards a course. The main pillars of mobilisation are:

- A course
- A sponsor of the course
- The target group
- The time frame

In Traditional Worldview and Mindset approach, mobilisation is skewed to the interests of a few people, who define their own course and use the target group at their own pace. This mindset leaves people feeling manipulated and used to achieve the narrow interests of the architects of such mobilisation. It fails to mobilise people for their own good. It, thus, uses incentives and other hooks to get a few leaders trapped and proceed to fulfill its narrow interests.

This kind of mobilisation is very common. African hotels and conferences are replete with platforms which harp on Africa's oral culture and plagiarizes Africa's intellectual property. It is not uncommon to hear an African here and an African there complain – on the global platform – how their ideas were stolen and stowed away in books. Like Esau of the Bible, who sold his birthright for a meal, Africa has sold her birthright for a meal. We have been stripped naked to be fed!

In Transformed Empowered Worldview and Mindset approach, mobilisation is for the benefit of the mobilised and is done in a consultative manner that upholds the dignity and personal space of the actors. It allows individual voices to be developed and expressed, corporately, on relevant platforms. It actively seeks to build on the identity and mission bias of the partners and harness and leverage resources to serve the greater interests of the target group and community.

It is time to redeem Africa's fortunes on the global market by going for what is rightfully her place. It is time for Africa's leaders to take stock of the state of their countries and make hard choices. Dambisa Moyo has said it well in her book *Dead Aid*. That Aid has not done Africa much good and it is time to rethink its architecture. Christian Impact Mission has mobilised a community and is aware of Dambisa's frustration. We are aware that development models of the past, championed by Western agencies, were well-intentioned, but they failed to be of much help. They actually ended up being harmful. Drawn into a land of hunger and despair, where death was just around the bend on a daily basis, CIM was moved to rally a community against the culture of defeat. The Holy Spirit was sent in to help us face the battle with the determined demonic foes – then to mobilise the people around the new concept of irrigation agriculture. We systematically dismantled the cultural altars as the Lord gave us one victory after another. The people of Yatta watched in awe as a once cursed land of death turned into a land of bumper harvest, where the name of the Lord was proclaimed without fear – because the witches were defeated.

Ongoing Training in Yatta

At the heart of mobilisation is the need to facilitate cohesion and harness existing systems and structures that serve as enablers in community development. CIM believes that the conversation on community development does not start with a mere baseline on community assets and gaps, but with focused consideration of anthropological experiences, skills, attitudes, indigenous knowledge, values, worldview, mindset, culture, aspirations and the governance architecture of a people. Failure to consider these factors amounts to *cultural imperialism* that imposes the *development workers culture* on the host community, packaged as development.

Experience has taught us, at CIM, that sustainable community transformation must take into account and mobilise local structures and systems. In this regard, CIM has identified seven levels of government:

7 LEVELS OF GOVERNMENT:

- Individual
- Family
- Village
- Church
- Community
- Nation
- International community

a. Individual government

The *individual* is the building block of society and is surrounded by spiritual, psychological, mental, social and emotional systems that either place limitations on his or her progress and development or serve as enablers. A development agenda must seek to break the *limitations* and create an enabling environment for the individual to experience life in its fullness.

In Traditional Worldview and Mindset approach, development initiatives do not fully consider the needs of the individual in a holistic sense. This foundational failure, to recognize interconnectedness of the body and spirit, may lead to individuals being liberated in one area, but remain trapped in another. This hinders the growth and progress of community members and keeps them from exerting meaningful impact at the family and community level.

In Transformed Empowered Worldview and Mindset approach, development initiatives consider the needs of the individual in a holistic sense. There is recognition of the interconnectedness of the body and spirit and care is taken to

Mobilisation Philosophy—127

mobilise systems and structures to liberate the individual and equip him or her to foster progress and growth and exert a meaningful impact at a family and community level.

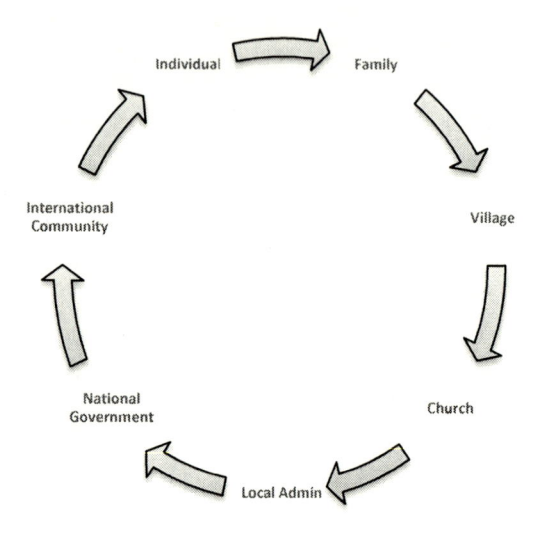

Individual → Family → Village → Church → Local Admin → National Government → International Community → Individual

Community Structures: Churches, Elders, Associations

The *total* needs of an individual are addressed in an integrated manner, aimed at enhancing life in its fullness. This means the individual is reconciled to God, to self, to others and to the environment; and acts as an agent of transformation in the community. This is the *utongoi approach* – a concept used by CIM to refer to a transformed leader who gets liberated to become a liberator in the community.

b. Family government

The family is an environment upon which the society is built. Through strengthening of relevant family systems, roles and responsibilities are clearly articulated; and leadership and other life skills are built for a healthy society to emerge.

In Traditional Worldview and Mindset approach, only a segment of the family is mobilised. Programmes are designed to address the needs of this segment without regard to the impact on the other segments. Such programmes include girl-child programmes, which have focused on the girl-child and created a crisis in the end, when the empowered girl-child grows up and cannot get an equally well-equipped boy-child to marry.

In Transformed Empowered Worldview and Mindset approach, the whole family is mobilised and *programmes* are designed to address the needs of the whole family. In Africa, family is a household unit that brings together relatives and each person that lives in the home. This household is structured to enhance family-cohesion and function – with various members playing specific roles and responsibilities.

Agnes' *metaphor* best captures the family government structure, using the civil government model of the President, Prime Minister, Cabinet and Civil Servants. The husband is the President, the wife is the Prime Minister, the children are the Cabinet Secretaries and the workers are the Civil Servants. She came up with this model to demonstrate the need for harmony in a home if transformation of the mind was to be achieved.

This became necessary because the Yatta we came to was a land where men and women lived like total strangers. Women were regarded lower than male children. Aware this mindset was going to be problematic for full realisation of the CIM dream, Agnes thought things through and came up with a model patterned after the then coalition government in Kenya, where the President and prime Minister were equals.

Looking back today, we consider the remarkable success of the family unit in Yatta as one of CIM's greatest joys. As families came together, it became easier to mobilise them around the core goals of a life dedicated to God, a life of prosperity here on earth, and a life lived to witness to others.

The village, church, community, nation and the international community are the other *critical* levels of government members of a community have to learn to work with. Each level has a role to play in facilitating smooth development. History has, however, taught us that national and international actors have not been of great help, but that is not a reason to look down upon their efforts. Indeed, we have to be gracious by contextualising their Africa and realising some of the setbacks and misdiagnoses and false approaches deployed were not a product of ill-will; but a product of the enormity of a burden they had to carry without the benefit of a precedent to follow.

Who is to be Mobilised?
This is the next logical question – who is to be mobilised? In any African community, we have come to realise, based on our experience in Yatta, that transformation replaced old structures

with new ones. The hostile takeover that took place in Yatta when Christianity moved in turned systems upside-down and gave the community new institutions, new leaders and new ideas to work with. These were what needed to be mobilised.

a. Community structures: churches and elders and associations

In Traditional Worldview and Mindset approach, mobilisation targets select segments of society as direct beneficiaries of particular interventions. In many cases, such mobilisation does not respect particular cultural and practical sensitivities. In many development agencies, mobilisation under this mindset, avoids the church and other religious platforms, yet often these groups have sustainable community structures that could have been used in programme delivery.

Conversely, in other cases, mobilisation restricts itself within the church or faith community and does not deliberately seek to bring in other segments of society.

In Transformed Empowered Worldview and Mindset approach, mobilisation systematically targets various segments of society. It starts with the gatekeepers of the community who serve as stabilizers, enforcers of stability and determinants of what goes on in the community. These local gatekeepers include elders, local churches, associations, schools, tertiary institutions, research centres and other groups.

In this form of mobilisation, one key community structure needs extra mention – the local church. We need to look a little deeper into why it is critical to mobilise the local church:

- It is God's agent of transformation in society through which society is preserved.
- It is an abiding edifice in the community, with multiple opportunities of engagement – the trusted entity that is with the families and communities in moments of pain and joy.
- It is a permanent institution in the community that serves as the only reliable *strategic custodian* of sustainable transformation.
- It is interwoven beyond geographic boundaries, with a global capacity to network and leverage her resources.
- It has a value-system and worldview that serve as a catalyst to community transformation, affecting such major areas as work ethic, labour relations, community cohesion and view of the future.
- It is part of community structures, often times frail and in need to capacity-building and strengthening. Not to build and strengthen it would amount to discrimination of community structures.

Sadly, although the church is a central part of community life, an enduring institution with knowledge of what a community goes through – right from birth to burial – the local church has been kept away from development dialogue by development actors like the NGOs and government entities.

b. Age groups: children, youth, adults

In Traditional Worldview and Mindset approach, mobilisation of the youth is often on tokenism terms or for manipulation for political convenience. It is done without there ever being a serious commitment to foster inclusion in agenda-setting. Although groups and teams may claim to be youth-focused, youth are often missing on the decision-making table.

Children under the age of fourteen are further neglected in mobilisation efforts. If mobilisation were ever done at all, their caregivers, parents and guardians would be excluded on the strategy-formulation table.

In Transformed Empowered Worldview and Mindset approach, mobilisation efforts are informed by the interconnectivity of the various age groups and deliberate effort is made to bring their voices on the table. This view goes beyond child-participation to child-integration in the decision-making processes. The guiding principle is that if decisions are going to be made about that group, the group needs to be integrated in the decision-making process.

The African Youth Charter brings it out well when it says in its preamble:

> … convinced that Africa's greatest resource is its youthful population and that through their active and full participation, Africans can surmount the difficulties that lie ahead.

It is critical that any initiative aimed at transforming a community brings the youth on board. Due to their interconnectivity, any mobilisation of one target group must, of essence, also target the other groups as well. Youth-focused programmes, for example, should also target adults, who often are the determinants of resources and time available to the youth.

The skewed targeting of programmes like the girl-child focused interventions, for example, done to the exclusion of the boy-child, have often resulted in skewed emphasis and denied the empowered girl-child an opportunity to deal with an equally empowered boy-child, resulting in continuous disequilibrium.

c. Gender: men, women

As an initial step in the design of community-based programmes, community dynamics such as structure and hierarchy, power structures and relations, decision-making patterns, and the differing roles of women and men, have to be considered. These constructs are often embedded in the community's culture and gender definitions.

While not exhausting discussions on gender, our purpose here is to make us realize there is a strong impact of gender and culture on community development. Effort needs to be made to interrogate gender definitions in a context and embrace progressive thought that empowers and mobilises the full capacity and potential of men and women in development.

In Traditional Worldview and Mindset approach, gender is restricted to mean women. In this mobilisation, women and girls are excluded from decision tables. Decisions are made for them. In the mostly patriarchal societies, men-headed households place undue pressure on men to carry the burdens of the families and fail to tap into the wisdom, experience and expertise presented by women, which would have provided a solution.

According to existing studies in this area, in most communities in Africa, women are dominated by men through patriarchal power, which has been a traditional and historical privilege for men. This also means that by perpetuating a male-dominated society, women and men have a relationship which is unequal. Consequently, society fails to reap the full benefits of God's design in which men and women walk as one in fulfilling their mission and mandate given at creation.

In Transformed Empowered Worldview and *Mindset* approach, gender issues are given equal attention in the decision-making processes, from design to implementation and to evaluation of development programmes. Gender is not assumed to refer to women, but to what it is as a *social construct* of females and males. Gender *mainstreaming* promotes harmony and partnership in addressing communal opportunities, threats and challenges.

Programmes and projects undertaken under this mindset conduct *gender-analysis* in community analysis or diagnosis. This analysis helps women and men redefine their relationship in a mutually beneficial way. It helps us gain an understanding of how people interact with each other, how they exchange information, how members of opposite sexes interact with each other, and the differences between the gender roles of women and men in the community.

In Yatta, we came to learn that the different roles women and men play in society, and the benefits that come with those roles, differ tremendously from culture to culture and have different values attached to them. Gender systems define attributes, ways of relating, hierarchies of decision-making, privileges, sanctions and space in which women and men are organised. If a development programme is to succeed, it has to take into account the prevailing cultural ways of a people – in relation to matters of gender.

Spurred to Urgency by Death

The story of the death of the woman in Yatta was carried by a local newspaper. While for many Kenyans it was the sad story of a mother who died of hunger in the distant lands of the east, for Agnes and I it was a wakeup call. As we mobilised the Yatta community to stop dependence on *mwolyo*, we rallied gospel artists in Kenya, led by Mercy Masika, our daughter, to round up funds for the community. The effort netted two million shillings and people were fed, but we knew we had to go beyond a one-time drive for food – Yatta needed liberation.

It is regrettable that it took the death of a mother to get us fired up, but we take comfort in the fact that the painful death didn't happen in vain. Because of it, CIM has implemented a *rigorous* programme that lays emphasis on identification of community priorities, its missing gaps, resource potential, external and internal barriers, indigenous technologies, experiences and knowledge. It fosters community identity, participation and ownership.

Emphasis has also been laid on community development. We have guided the Yatta community to look from within for the resources before looking for external donors. The focus is to lead them to become donors and economic generators rather than seekers of *mwolyo*. CIM's role has been to balance the need for strategic external resources with the long-term goal of eradication of all forms of donor dependence – which is one of the causes of sustained poverty in Kenya.

Walking through the paths of the village today, one can't help but notice LIFE in the people. They are empowered to attain food security and create wealth – and are now able to fend for themselves. All these are as a result of our desire, and the initiative, to see fulfillment of the biblical promise of abundant life according to John 10:10.

Operation Mwolyo Out has saved Yatta!

Reflection
a. In community mobilisation, what are some examples of mobilisations done for the benefit of the mobiliser and not the community?
b. We've established that mobilisation needs to focus on the seven levels of government. Which are these levels and what are their relevance for development agencies, county governments, and national governments?
c. Looking at the Yatta miracle, how mobilisation was done, what are some lessons that we can learn from this model?

CHAPTER FIVE

MOBILISATION FOR 1-ACRE RULE MIRACLE

The skepticism was palpable. We had called a meeting of the people at a time death and despair had gripped the land. The cows were dead, the goats reduced to digging for roots with their teeth and children were faced with the danger of death – for those lucky to survive the dry spell. In a home not too far from mine, a woman had died, left behind her toddler twins, for lack of food. All over the land, there was a sense that the gods had conspired to eliminate a village. I could tell that even the great sorcerers and rainmakers were as confounded by this aggressive phenomenon as the rest of us.

As I already mentioned in a previous chapter, the scale of death in Yatta touched a raw nerve in my heart. I couldn't understand why the Christian community in Kenya – and around the world – couldn't respond to the urgent pleas of the people. How many more deaths were Christians waiting to see before it was too much? How many children had to die? How many women had to wet their pillows at night as their emaciated children suckled on breasts that were as dry as the riverbeds across the land? Where was Christ in the deafening silence of the people who filled fancy religious institutions on Sunday mornings to praise the Almighty God? Was Christianity dead?

In the face of death and despair, however, I had no time to sit still and seek answers to those questions; what I had time for was to urgently save lives. This was the reason I turned to Mercy and other artists to raise funds, through gospel music, to feed the people. I didn't want to see one more child dead. I didn't want to hear of another mother killed. And I didn't want the nonsense of hearing about culture and ancestors and what we could do and couldn't do. If those ancestors were going to kill me as I saved people, so be it. Enough was enough!

Mercy and her group raised two million shillings and it gave us a great start in saving lives, but I knew that the approach was not a sustainable one. In a land as dry as Yatta – regarded as one of the poorest communities in Kenya – what we were experiencing was just but another among the waves of hunger that gripped the land; another was coming. Aware of this, it became urgent for us to think of a sustainable solution to the endemic hunger problem in the land. It was now evident that reliance on *mwolyo*, and on a donor community that prescribed solutions to a situation whose anthropological background it wasn't conversant with, was sure to lead to more deaths in the future. Yatta needed to be saved now!

Looking back, I realise that not many people saw the problem in Yatta for what it really was. I already said it was one of a deep spiritual warfare, but that was just one of the problems. The other was broader in scope than Yatta. If you peruse the newspapers of the time, what you will see was extensive coverage of the situation as it evolved. The graphic images of a land cursed, a people dying, a donor community in a tailspin, were on the pages of newspapers – yet there was hardly any coordinated response from sources one hoped help could come from. Yatta was left alone in her hour of need.

I have to confess that one of the driving forces in me – at the time – was deep anger. I was angry at my fellow Christians for talking too much about salvation yet people were dying; I was angry at civic authorities who appeared clueless and greedy in the face of turmoil; I was angry at my fellow Kenyans for abandoning their brothers and sisters in their hour of need; and I was angry at the donor community for failing to move in enough relief to save the people of Yatta. That anger spurred me into action, but more importantly, it made me look beyond the immediate problem and caused me to look for a lasting solution. The gospel meant nothing to Yatta if it left people in a state where poverty, death and despair ruled the day.

On the day we first introduced the concept of water pans, I could tell most women gathered appeared skeptical. First of all, there was the fear of disturbing the ancestors, a taboo nobody was ready to mess with. Then there was the fact that nobody was strong enough to start digging a hole big enough to hold even a few gallons of water, leave alone a deep water pan. We, however, explained how it would work. Basing our approach on the concept of merry-go-round, which they were already familiar with, we introduced the concept of donated labour. On a given day, women were to come together and dig a water pan in one home, then they would go to the next home the next day. This process played out until a number of homes were covered.

We then introduced the concept of planting different plants so that in one farm, there were various yields. We urged people to plant maize, beans, vegetables, fruits and even bring back cows, goats and sheep. I could tell, as we embarked on this process, that some people feared a backlash from seething gods. They remained jittery, tentative and guarded, ready to flee at the first manifestation of trouble. But we were not about to give up; we remained on course, waking up each day to dig water pans, plant crops and invite more people into the programme.

Seven months after we started, at the height of the dry spell, the people of Yatta witnessed the first miracle. While villages in the greater eastern region waited for the rains to start planting, the people of Yatta were ready to harvest – and it was going to be one of the biggest harvests ever seen.

Agnes tells me that one lady, when she saw what was going on, asked her what they would do with the food. I am not a man of deep emotions, but a question like that drew my tears. In just a couple of months we had gone from a village on the throes of devastation to one where women now wondered what they would do with excess food. We were, however, not ready to sit on our laurels because there were still too many families that had not joined us. We had to bring them in under the banner of Operation Mwolyo Out.

As the programme developed, we noted a need to teach our people how to maximize usage of available space. This is what became known as the 1-Acre-Rule Miracle.

The 1-Acre-Rule-Miracle
The best place to begin this discussion would be to define the 1-Acre-Rule Miracle. This is one of the concepts that has revolutionized agriculture in Yatta and created millionaires where there once was grinding poverty. We have, thus, realized that Africa's agriculture can and needs to be redeemed. The utilization of Africa's resources needs to be maximized on the agricultural value-chain. This is the importance of the 1-Acre-Rule-Miracle. That is its real definition.

In Traditional Worldview and Mindset approach, there is a tendency to focus on quantity without quality. Households till large tracts of land and thinly spread farm inputs like seeds, fertilizer, water, and other resources, leading to low yields and returns. Due to this lack of strategic optimization of resources on the land, families gradually erode their farming capacity and experience food insecurity and diminished livelihoods. This is a great challenge, especially in arid areas like Yatta, where water is a major challenge.

The practice, among most farmers in arid lands, is to spread meager farm inputs over large tracts of land, with *resulting* poor performance and minimal yields. The absence of a systematic approach leads to what I refer to as the *kiundutho* mindset – the mindset of lacking a plan and order in life and work.

For example, before the OMO project came to Yatta, farmers were tilling an average of six to ten acres of land and harvesting only three to six bags. This meager harvest was later sold at a throwaway price to greedy middlemen in order to take care of immediate needs, after which most families would return to depending on relief food from the government or NGOs. Through the principle of 1-Acre-Rule Miracle, farmers became able to select the most optimal size of land for the farm inputs.

In Transformed Empowered Worldview and *Mindset* approach, efforts are made to ensure households take up optimal land space in which to experience food security and enhanced livelihood. This is the concept of the 1-Acre-Rule, where communities are taught how to use land optimally and grow crops organically.

Through systematic planning and organisation, land is managed in ways that optimize use of water and other resources. This is achieved by planting various types of crops on a small piece of land – in ways that address food security of the household, conserves the environment, builds livelihoods through high-value crops, and positions the household on an economic development trajectory through value-addition programmes.

The standard one-acre piece of land is divided into various portions geared towards addressing food security and wealth-creation, among other needs. Once the farmer has optimized use of the one acre, the size of land under use can be expanded progressively, depending on a farmer's capacity at any one time. The concept seeks to make maximum use of resources on the farm and help develop a model farm that can fit the various sizes of land. It seeks to demonstrate the power of organisation and systematic thinking in how land is managed.

Apportioning the 1 Acre

Today it happens with ease, when farmers in Yatta apportion their land for maximum output, but there was a time it wasn't that easy. We spent days in training, showing farmers how to apply the 1-acre rule. We stressed the fact that it wasn't about the size of a land, but the arithmetic of its division. Here is a sample of a plan we worked with:

a. Food security – ¼ Acre

About quarter of an acre was set aside for producing staple food for the family. This was achieved through technologies like Zai Pits, farming God's way (zero tillage), and moist gardens, among others. Through research and innovation, the most appropriate crops for the semi-arid Yatta area were selected in partnership with institutions like universities and relevant research stations.

In our experience, not only was the size of land a challenge, but the land tillage method of ploughing was not suitable for the soils in the arid and semi-arid lands (ASAL). This was because it exposed the soils to being washed away during the short but torrential rains experienced in the region. The rains carried away the top soil, leaving the remaining soil infertile, thin, gullied and unproductive.

The first area of intervention in assisting this community to realise food security, therefore, was to influence the method of land tillage. The zai pits method proved to be the most suitable. This method, so new to the Yatta people, increased production per acreage tremendously. The water in the pans was able to support crops such as maize and beans to maturity in the zai pits, thus increasing production.

Today, farmers know that the benefits of these pits are many: they are effective in reducing soil erosion, maintaining humidity and fastening the maturity of crops. The pits are also ideal in areas where rain is erratic and minimal. In Yatta, for example, even if it rains for just a month, people are able to harvest food as the pits conserve water and they are able to focus irrigation into these pits – from the water in the pans.

A plant is not a camel that it can store water for long, and neither is it a fish that requires swimming in water – providing enough water to the plant in the pit is enough to help it grow.

b. Livelihoods – ¾ Acre

This was further divided into:

- **High-value Crops ¼ Acre**

A quarter of an acre was apportioned for high-value crops, where appropriate high-value crops like turmeric, ginger, garlic, *capsicum*, tomatoes, onions, carrots, passion fruits and mangoes were identified and planted.

After food security needs were addressed, the community was mobilised to adopt high-value crops for its livelihood. High-value crops for a given region, we know today, should be selected in partnership with centres of excellence and leading research institutions and colleges; back then, I can only *conclude* we were guided by the Holy Spirit!

The Yatta project has grown to a level where it has a significant seed bank – made available to farmers in other ASAL areas. We believe that the secret to financial freedom in rural areas is to grow these high-value crops in significant acreage, and in a systematic manner, as stipulated by the model.

- **Livestock – ½ Acre**

About half an acre was dedicated to livestock and poultry keeping. Through the creation of a cycle, the three components formed a miraculous symbiotic relationship in which livestock farming provided manure for crop farming and crop farming provided fodder for livestock. This reduced *wastage* and created systems that turned out to be self-supporting.

The Lord was talking to us!

Components of the 1-Acre-Rule Miracle

The key components of 1-Acre Rule Miracle are:

- Access to sufficient water
- Using appropriate adaptation technologies
- Market-driven agriculture

To make sense out of this foundational concept, we need to discuss the listed matters in a systematic manner. We start with access to sufficient water.

1. **Access to sufficient water**

Efforts should be made to access water through appropriate water-harvesting techniques. Good water harvesting mitigates flush flooding and run-off that is common in the ASAL areas. It reduces demand on underground water reservoirs and makes available potable water with low salinity in some of the areas. Properly handled, it could also help transform the vegetation through the capillarity action, in the root system. The water harvesting techniques include:

a. **Roof catchment**

This is, perhaps, the cheapest method. It makes use of high-up areas and makes water readily available, in proximate terms, to the place where it is needed for domestic use. Through the use of gutters, water is directed from rooftops of buildings and structures into reservoirs. The larger the surface area of a roof, the more the amount of water likely to be collected. Many city planners have integrated water-harvesting in their architecture.

b. **Water pans**

The science of constructing water pans is simple. Two critical factors to watch are: digging the water pan in such a way that active surface for evaporation is reduced, and positioning the water pan in such a way that it has an overflow valve or outlet; and that the inlet is not direct but goes through diversions that help reduce sedimentation in the water pan.

Working with households in Yatta, more than one thousand water pans have been constructed and equipped to provide water for multiple domestic use, dairy farming and irrigation.

Through the use of such technologies as solar power, water so harvested can be pumped into water resources located at places with a high water head and allowing it to flow, through gravity, to other areas of the farm.

c. Furrows or ridges

A mere construction of furrows and ridges has the capacity to trap and direct run-off or overflow water from water pans and other locations and be made available to the animals and plants in strategic areas.

d. Forest or tree cover harvesting

With proper forest cover, certain sections of land will provide a large continuous sheet of foliage cover that traps the rain water and allows water so harvested to percolate slowly into the ground. This feeds into streams and replenishes the *underground* water reservoirs like springs, boreholes and wells.

2. Appropriate technologies

By technology, we are focusing on how techniques, methods, processes, varieties and breeds are employed to put knowledge in research and development into use and help improve the quality of life and business delivery. On the table in the next page, we look at farming types in ASAL areas and wetlands in relation to appropriate or applicable technology.

	ASAL Areas	Wetlands
Fish Farming	Raised Fish Pond Vermi Composting (African worms)	Raised Fish Pond Vermi Composting (African worms)
Livestock	Cross Breeding Hydroponics Zero Grazing	Cross-Breeding Hydroponics Zero Grazing
Poultry	Cross- Breeding (Broilers, Free Range) Chicken Coop	Cross- Breeding (Broilers, Free Range) Chicken Coop
Crop Production	Mulching Drip Irrigation Zai Pits Farming God's Way Hydroponics Moist Gardens Charcoal Cooler Solar Dryer Composting Vermi Composting (for producing folia fertilizer)	Mulching Zai Pits Farming God's Way Hydroponics Charcoal Cooler Solar Dryer Composting Vermi Composting (for producing folia fertilizer)
Processing	Charcoal Cooler Bakery Solar Dryer Fireless Cooker Incubators Soil Sampling and Testing Aquaponics	

Farming types in ASAL and Wet Areas

The following are some of the appropriate technologies that are useful in implementing the 1-Acre principle of farming:

- **Drip irrigation**

This technology requires less manpower, provides consistent water supply in optimal amounts and is very useful in high-value crop production in ASAL areas.

Rev. Geoffrey Mulu, one of the CIM members at a drip irrigation Demonstration farm in Yatta

- **Cross-breeding**

Cross-breeding helps in enhancing productivity through careful and deliberate selection of gene pool.

Boa and Galla goats for cross-breeding at the CIM Centre, Yatta.

- **Vermi composting**

This technology is used in producing folia fertilizer for organic farming. The night crawlers, or African worms, serve as decomposition agents, and also act as food for fish.

Bishop Masika demonstrates Vermi Composting Process to a seminar participant at the CIM Centre, Yatta

- **Solar dryer**

Solar dryer is a low-cost, post-harvest handling technology that helps increase the shelf life of food and fruit.

Community members undergoing training at CIM Centre in Yatta on how to use a solar dryer

- **Bakery**

A bakery is a value-addition technology that provides an expanded platform for agricultural crops value-chain and agri-nutrition, especially for school-going children.

Deputy Governor, Machakos County when he officially opened the CIM Bakery and Value Addition Plant in June 2014

- **Moist garden**

Moist garden is a technology that requires little space and less water. It is useful for raising vegetables, especially in kitchen gardens.

Moist farming in Yatta

Zai pit farm: French beans planted in between maize

- **Zai Pits**

According to *Wikipedia*, Zai is a farming technique to dig pits in the soil during the preseason to catch water and collect compost. The technique is traditionally used to restore degraded drylands and increase soil fertility. The pits are useful for retaining water and other inputs and making them readily available for the crops throughout the production period. In Yatta, we came to realize that through these adaptive, water-harvesting technologies, our arid community could transform agricultural production and lead us to total emancipation from the realm of *mwolyo* and lack of human dignity.

3. Market-driven agriculture

Before engaging in production under the 1-Acre Rule Miracle, it is important that a farmer conducts market research to establish the demand for various possible farming options. This will help create a market-driven business that balances supply with demand. The linkages should be established both with the local and the external markets, through business and capacity-building. It is important that effort is made to strengthen systems at individual, village and community level. This should be done in ways that build synergies and cohesion needed for optimum utilisation of resources in the value-chain; for the benefit of all in the chain. In the long run, this is what *provides* a competitive advantage in the market.

4. Agri-nutrition

In the 1-Acre Rule Miracle, it is important that a systematic assessment of the nutritional needs of *households* and *communities* be carried out in order to allow the communities to grow and rear, not only what the market wants, but what addresses their nutritional gaps as well. This is why CIM's 1-Acre Rule Miracle seeks to address the issue of communities producing the right foods in the right quantities and the right quality. Given the malnutrition status for Kenya, where at provincial level estimates show that Eastern (42.6%) and Coast (36.0%) have higher proportions of stunted children, while Nairobi (27.8%) and Central (30.0%) provinces have lower proportions compared with the national level estimate, this is critical.

Benefits of the 1-Acre-Rule Miracle

There are lessons that can only be learned by *seeing* and *feeling*, not by hearing. In once-semi-arid Yatta, liberated farmers have seen and felt the impact of practical Christianity in the way irrigation agriculture has created a community of believers. If you were to ask them the benefits of the 1-Acre Rule Miracle, they would speak from experience.

a. **Food-security**

Like the farmers of Yatta, CIM holds dear the truth that the 1-Acre Rule Miracle is the answer for food security – especially in ASAL areas that are still food-insecure and depend on relief aid. With increased partnership with government agencies and the development sector, the capacity of communities can be adequately increased to address all food-security components of availability, access, utilization and stability.

b. **Improved nutrition**

Through systematic assessment of the nutritional needs of households and communities, the 1-Acre-Rule Miracle allows communities to grow and rear what addresses their nutritional gaps, in quantity and quality. Through training and advocacy in communities producing and consuming these nutritional foods, their nutritional status and health are improved.

c. Wealth-creation

In providing cascading layers of intervention – from food security, livelihoods, value-addition and cottage industries – the 1-Acre-Rule Miracle provides a seamless flow in harnessing of community resources for economic empowerment.

Peter Mutiso is a community member in Yatta, where the CIM Model was first implemented. Peter successfully implemented the 1-Acre-Rule Miracle and has become a successful, food-secure farmer. When he worked in Nairobi, as a bread vendor, he earned a commission of three thousand shillings per month. To cope with the high cost of living, he was forced to stay with five other people in a *mabati* or iron sheet room.

When Peter heard of the miraculous changes taking place in Yatta, he chose to come back home. He had twenty shillings on arrival. With that money, he bought 50g of *sukuma wiki* or kales seeds. After digging a water pan, he planted the *sukuma wiki* on a ¾-acre portion of family land. Peter sold *sukuma wiki* for four months. From the proceeds, he bought beans, which he stored. After a month, the prices of beans improved. Peter sold the beans and made fifty thousand shillings, which he used to expand his farm, bringing on board livestock, poultry, fruits and other horticultural crops. From ¾ acres, he increased his farming to eight acres, with an income of between 80,000 and

200,000 shillings per month. Like Peter, Yatta men who had fled to the city and towns, following the desperate situation, have now come back and are growing food for family consumption – and are making good money from the sweat of their hands. Most of the men came back when Agnes launched Operation Men Back, a campaign driven by Yatta women to bring back their husbands.

d. Job-creation

With increasing levels of unemployment, due to unreliable and scarce rainfall, the 1-Acre Rule Miracle creates employment opportunities by shifting mindset from rain-fed agriculture to conservation farming methods. It also provides households with a systematic approach to making optimum utilisation of resources. Through accelerated production and value-addition processes, several employment opportunities are created for various persons on the value-chain. In Yatta, there are more than six thousand households fully engaged in their farms and job opportunities are opening up. This has provided opportunities for men, women and youth to be engaged in gainful employment. The value-addition bakery in the CIM farm, for example, has brought many people onto the value-chain, including producers, suppliers, distributors, merchandisers and retailers.

Bernard Mutua Katuku, a businessman in Yatta, is one such youth who has been impacted by the 1-Acre Rule Miracle. He started selling Yatta Bread on four motorcycles – selling one thousand loaves per day. In just six months, Bernard grew his capacity to eleven motorcycles. If this is not job-creation, what is?

e. Preparing for retirement

In an environment where many households have depended on employment as a source of income, career transition choices and decisions are heavily influenced by upkeep concerns. At the point of retirement, many households are ill-prepared to face the prospects of living off inadequate pension, with some making wrong investment choices. Through the 1-Acre-Rule Miracle, they are taught to grow their investment gradually and systematically as their competencies and capacities grow in preparation for retirement.

f. Climate-change adaptation

Due to changing weather patterns – with a heavy impact on biodiversity and increased vulnerabilities, in which rainfall is unpredictable and reliance on rain-fed agriculture no longer tenable, the 1-Acre Rule Miracle provides a reliable shift into continuous farming through water-harvesting technologies and conservation agriculture. Water is made use of in optimal amounts. This shields farmers from the otherwise debilitating effects of climate change.

Exporting the 1-Acre Rule Miracle

We have lit the candle!

Bondo

In partnership with the religious institutions in Bondo, Siaya County, CIM trained community members on the 1-Acre-Rule Miracle and is monitoring implementation of the model.

East Pokot

At the invitation of the people of East Pokot, through elders and the local administration, CIM embarked on the journey of working with the community to find long-term solutions to endemic food insecurity, in the face of *relentless* climate-change and associated challenges.

Tanzania

In partnership with World Vision Tanzania – which facilitated community members from Tanzania – CIM trained more than one thousand staff and community members between August 2012 and October 2014. We focused on the comprehensive CIM Development Model, including the empowered biblical worldview approach and the 1-Acre Rule Miracle in Yatta. The training was followed by field mentorship programmes, conducted by CIM team, aimed at supporting the community and World Vision Tanzania staff in implementing the model.

The impact of this training is observable in the accelerated business output and livelihood transformation documented by World Vision Tanzania: development of more than seven model biogas plants, construction of over five hundred water pans, increased diversity in agro-products, modest increase in empowered savings groups, establishment of a 500-ha model Farmer Managed Natural Regeneration (FMNR), formation of more than 800 Commercial producer groups, more than 100 energy saving cooking stoves, and sustainable community social responsibility. And as observed elsewhere, the CIM Model – hinged on a transformed and empowered worldview and mindset – has been seen to achieve great impact in a significantly reduced time-frame and cost. Indeed, during *mentorship* visits, to support those who attended CIM's development model training, in Yatta, our team often encounters many transformation stories. One such story is that of Mzee Shabaan Musa, a Muslim leader in Ayasanda. Mzee Musa narrated his experience, following the training in Yatta. Upon listening to us, he became convinced that true religion was one that helped bring development and influenced livelihoods through transformation. As a spiritual leader, the elderly man embarked on being a model of transformation – in line with CIM's leadership and mobilisation model. Within a month of the training, his home became a picture of transformation. He had a vegetable garden, a moist garden, a 20-ft. bore hole, twenty chicks and a water pan. Yatta had come to Tanzania!

Rwanda

In partnership with the religious institutions in Rwanda, and World Vision Rwanda, the CIM Development Model, especially the 1-Acre Rule Miracle, has had an *impact* in Rwanda. CIM has conducted training – in Yatta – for religious institution leaders and World Vision staff from Rwanda. CIM has also held follow up trips and vision conferences and seminars in Rwanda for momentum building on empowered transformational development. This has made the *transformation* movement take root in World Vision programme areas, in partnership with the government.

Reflection

a. Looking at how the 1-Acre-Rule Miracle is designed, how can county and national governments, and the humanitarian sector, use it in helping create jobs for the youth and meet the nutritional needs of school-going children?

b. What policies and processes can county and national governments *implement* to increase maximum utilisation of resources and creation of commercial villages and centres?

c. Increasingly, industrial agriculture is being blamed for industrial effluents and degradation of environment. How can the 1-Acre Rule Miracle be an answer to this?

6 CHAPTER SIX

GENDER IN DEVELOPMENT

Agnes makes fun of the way Operation Men Back was started, but it is only to make a critical point about one of the greatest transformations to ever take place in Yatta. She says that in the early days, when I went to Yatta and she remained in Nairobi, word reached her that the women in Yatta had "taken" her husband. Afraid of losing me, she decided to hurry things up a bit and join me. When she finally came, she says, she found humble people who were no threat to her at all. That's a line that draws huge laughter whenever we are at trainings. She follows it up by saying it was the reason she decided to bring back the men of the community.

In what Agnes later dubbed Operation Men Back, we began one of the most ambitious transformations of all. I grew up in Ukambani and knew how women were regarded in the community. I knew how men looked down on their mothers, their wives and their daughters. It wasn't spitefulness or disrespect; it was just a cultural thing that made even the smallest boy occupy a place more elevated than a woman.

While in developed nations women were at the point of driving legislation and pushing a powerful narrative in demand for fair treatment and equality in all aspects of life, in Yatta our women were trapped in time warp, unaware they were supposed to be equal to men in anything. They gladly accepted a status quo in which they could neither inherit property nor make any key decisions once a husband was dead. Indeed, it was as if the death of a husband ended her life as well – all she remained to do in the world was wait for the day of her death so she could be reunited with her husband in the other realm.

CIM got into the picture and fought this cultural baggage. We were keenly aware of the fact that if women and men didn't work together in reforming their minds – so that together the community could be transformed – we were not going to make any gains. I remain grateful to Agnes, for her foresight, in sensing the need to bring the community's men into the picture early enough that they could participate and take ownership of the transformation in Yatta.

As I pointed out in an earlier chapter, in most settings the term gender normally refers to women. In the field of development, however, we depart from that simplistic approach and bring to the surface complexities that reflect the weight of the term. Obviously then, the place to begin this discussion would be to define the term gender. What is it?

Gender Defined

According to UNAID, gender refers to widely shared ideas and expectations or norms about women and men – ideas about typically feminine and masculine characteristics and abilities, expectations about how women and men should behave in various situations. These ideas and expectations are learned from families, friends, opinion leaders, religious and cultural institutions, schools, the workplace and the media. They reflect and influence the different roles, for example, social status, economic and political power of women and men in society.

The different roles women and men play, and the benefits that come with those roles, differ tremendously from culture to culture and have different values attached to them. Such constructs shape gender practices, symbols, representation norms and social values.

Gender systems define attributes, ways of relating, hierarchies of decision-making, privileges, sanctions and space in which women and men are organised.

As with culture, gender definitions change over time. Such change is driven by many factors. Cultural change occurs as communities and households respond to social and economic shifts associated with globalization, with new technologies, environmental pressures, armed conflict, development projects, and any new dynamics with an impact on life.

New cultural definitions are formed through a process in which some segments of society promote change through advocacy and example, while others resist it. In other words, societies are not homogeneous and no assumptions can be made about a consensus on *cultural values*.

As an initial step in the design of community-based programmes, community dynamics such as structure and hierarchy, power structures and relations, decision-making patterns, and the differing roles of women and men, have to be considered. These constructs are often embedded in the community's culture and gender definitions. Any entrant into a community such as Yatta, who fails to take into account these dynamics, is bound to raffle feathers and will face stiff opposition. In the early days, *before being accepted* as a friend, the wise approach is to work within the existing cultural framework, then later on dismantle it to give way for transformation in worldview and mindset. This is the common sense approach.

Relationship between Culture and Gender

While not exhausting discussions on gender, our purpose here is to challenge us to realize there is a strong impact of gender and culture on community development and effort needs to be made to *interrogate* gender definitions in a context and embrace progressive thought that empowers and mobilises the full capacity and potential of men and women in development.

If it is "cultural" is it unquestioned?

As suggested in the point above, cultural values are continually being reinterpreted in response to new needs and conditions. Some values are reaffirmed in this process, while others are challenged as no longer appropriate.

Concerns about culture are frequently raised in relation to initiatives for gender equality in development cooperation. In some cases, programme officers or partners are concerned that promotion of gender equality would interfere with local culture and therefore feel gender equality should not be promoted for *ethical* reasons. In other cases, the cultural values of a particular area are described as a major constraint on efforts for gender equality – and therefore action is considered to be difficult for practical reasons.

When we talk about *culture*, we often refer to intellectual and creative products: literature, music, drama, and even painting. Another meaning of the term *culture* is to describe the beliefs and practices of another society, particularly where these are seen as closely linked with tradition or religion.

Culture, however, is more than that. Culture is part of the fabric of every society, including our own. It shapes the way things are done and our understanding of why it should be so. This more *comprehensive* approach is proposed in the definition of culture adopted at the World Conference on Cultural Policies (Mexico, 1982), and is used in ongoing discussions on culture and development. It states:

> Culture... is... the whole complex of distinctive spiritual, material, intellectual and emotional features that characterize a society or a social group. It includes not only arts and letters, but also modes of life, the fundamental rights of the human being, value systems, traditions and beliefs.

Expectations about attributes and behaviors appropriate to women or men, and about the relations between women and men, are largely shaped by culture. Gender *identities* and gender *relations* too are critical aspects of culture because they shape the way daily life is lived in the family, but also in the wider community and the workplace.

Gender – like race or ethnicity – functions as an organising principle for society because of the cultural meaning given to being male or female. This is evident in the division of labour according to gender. Indeed, in most societies there are clear patterns of *women's work* and *men's work*, both in the household and in the wider community – and cultural explanations of why this should be so. The patterns and the explanations differ among societies and change over time. For instance, in the African setting, it was the women, in most communities, who were solely left to play the role of putting up the housing facility for the family. This is still evident in some communities like Maasai. This has since changed over time and men have currently taken over the role.

While the specific nature of gender relations varies among societies, the general pattern is that women have less personal autonomy, fewer resources at their disposal, and limited influence over the decision-making processes that shape their societies and their own lives. This pattern of disparity, based on gender, is both a human rights and a development issue. And indeed, as we established in Yatta, it is at the heart of failure or success of an effort to transform a community.

Gender and Worldviews

In Traditional Worldview and Mindset approach, *gender* is assumed to mean women. In this worldview, the associated social construct that spells out roles and responsibilities is designed in favour of either men or women. However, it is often women that are disadvantaged. In either matriarchal or patriarchal settings, there is little integration of collective gifts and competencies in moving society forward. Under this construct, women and girls are excluded from decision-making. Decisions are made for them. Indeed, in the patriarchal society, *men-headed* households place undue pressure on men to carry the burdens of the families. They fail to tap into the *wisdom*, experience and expertise presented by women, which would have provided a solution.

According to existing studies in this area, in most communities in Africa, women are dominated by men through patriarchal power, which has been a traditional and historical privilege for men. This also means that by perpetuating a male-dominated society, women and men have a relationship which is unequal. Consequently, society fails to reap the full benefits of God's design, in which men and women walk as one in fulfilling their mission and mandate – given at creation.

In Transformed Empowered Worldview and Mindset approach, *gender* issues are given attention in decision-making processes, right from design to implementation, and to evaluation of development programmes. In this worldview, the social construct that spells out roles and responsibilities is designed in favour of *both* men and women. In either a matriarchal or a patriarchal setting, there is *deliberate* integration of collective gifts and competencies in moving society forward.

Gender is not assumed to be referring to women, but for what it is as a social construct of females and males. This gender *mainstreaming* promotes harmony and partnership in addressing community opportunities, challenges and threats. Programmes and projects undertaken under this mindset *deliberately* conduct gender analysis in community analysis or diagnosis.

This gender analysis helps women and men redefine their relationship in a mutually beneficial way. It makes us gain an understanding of how people interact with each other, how they exchange information, how members of opposite sexes interact with each other; and the difference between the gender roles of women and men in a community.

Gender-Sensitivity in Development

As CIM, our marching orders are a matter of *origins*. We follow in the Creator's footsteps as we uphold the loving nature of relationship He designed for a woman and a man as in Genesis 1:26-28 (KJV).

> And God said, Let us make man in our image, after our likeness: and let them have dominion over the fish of the sea, and over the fowl of the air, and over the cattle, and over all the earth, and over every creeping thing that creepeth upon the earth.
> [27] So God created man in his own image, in the image of God created he him; male and female created he them.

[28] And God blessed them, and God said unto them, Be fruitful, and multiply, and replenish the earth, and subdue it: and have dominion over the fish of the sea, and over the fowl of the air, and over every living thing that moveth upon the earth.

Sensitivity in gender considerations will include areas such as roles and *responsibilities*, relations and communications. When this is done effectively, programmes will address the real, practical, and strategic needs of women and men within an existing social construct. Change will, thus, not be threatening to *either* women or men because both sexes will have owned it. A common ground and understanding will have been established for effective couple relations and a meaningful family life. A new mindset will take root to enable redistribution of reproductive responsibilities and remove the present gap in equalities.

Integrating Gender in Community Development

As an initial step in the design of community-based programmes, community dynamics such as community structure and hierarchy, power structures and relations, decision-making patterns, and the differing roles of women and men, have to be considered. Associating the concept of gender with women alone often creates obstacles when addressing the role of partnership in development. Gender mainstreaming requires change in mindset and facilitates the solving of community problems, which promotes harmony and partnership between women and men.

As introduced in the chapter on mobilisation, CIM's Gender in Development programme – championed by Agnes – introduces this harmony in working relationships and roles, through the family *government* structure. It was because of gender inclusivity that Agnes started the very *successful* campaign Operation Men Back. I dare say that had we not brought men into the picture, ownership of the reform programme in Yatta would have been an exclusively women affair – it would have failed.

It didn't take us long to realise there was no *formula* for making integration of gender happen other than to painstakingly work at mindset change. We had to guide women and men into a place of comfort on gender matters, help them to engender a worldview of inclusivity in and out of the home. Our efforts have borne fruit and the community has immensely benefitted.

Benefits of Integrating Gender in Community Development

If we were to sum up the benefits of gender-integration in development in one word, that word would be Yatta. Based on our experiences in the arid land, we have noted that bringing men and women into a development programme:

- Helps to identify influential community members and resources for use in the project prior to developing specifics of the project.
- Helps to mobilise community members and encourages them to invest energy in organising labor and resources for their benefit.

- Ensures provision of services that women and men want and are appropriate for their circumstances.

Reflections

a. How can we ensure that in both the matriarchal and patriarchal settings, there is deliberate integration of collective gifts and competencies in moving society forward?

b. Looking at how the metaphor of civic government has been used to describe relationships within the family set up, what are some of the ways this could be used in the pre-marital counseling and civic education in shaping the architecture of society?

c. Looking at how far society has come in addressing gender issues, how can we benefit from this chapter in dealing with the distance left to be covered?

CHAPTER SEVEN

SECURING OUR YOUTH

I have to hit the ground running on this matter. According to a report by the African Union Commission, about 65% of the total population of Africa is below the age of 35 years, and more than 35% are between the ages of 15 and 35. This makes Africa the most youthful continent. By 2020, it is projected that out of 4 people, 3 will be on average 20 years old. The report goes further to state that the labour market in Africa receives about 10 million young African youth each year. These are staggering figures indeed, but they are reality.

Not too long ago, Agnes and I drove along the road into the CIM Centre in Yatta. We noted, as our truck crawled along the dusty entryway way, that the market place, which once upon a time teamed with idle youth, was deserted. There were just but a few of them – and most of those were either carrying out a form of trade, out to buy something or were on transit from another part of the village.

Yatta had become a village of busy youth, most of them engaged in productive farm work. The mindset had changed from one of idleness to one of work.

Our View of the Youth

Youth could be disaggregated into the rural and urban youth. The rural youth often face isolation and exclusion from access to land and production assets. Urban youth are also excluded from the decision-making process on the basis of age and limited experience. The resultant effect is that many of these youth are rendered *irrelevant*, with a high degree of vulnerability and dependence. Governments and other stakeholders must be deliberate in creating an enabling environment for the youth to access production assets and participate in decision-making processes. Two worldviews are critical in how we view youth in our time.

a. Unemployment vs. labour force

The Traditional Worldview and Mindset approach views the youth in relation to their state of unemployment. It treats this as a challenge to be faced, with promises made by many governments on how to tackle this challenge.

The Transformed Empowered Worldview and Mindset approach views youth as a workforce to be engaged. Deliberate efforts are made for the youth to be engaged – to move from being jobseekers to job creators. Peter Mutiso, of the 1-Acre-Rule Miracle, is one such youth who has become a job creator. Africa will start making great strides the day she stops lamenting over her youth as unemployed and starts mobilizing the youth as a workforce for Africa's deliverance.

CIM believes deliberate effort should be made to integrate the youth in community life. They should be drawn in as *participants* and *decision-makers* in the process. The challenge is not one of unemployment, but one of *un-engagement*.

The African Youth Charter brings it out well when it says, in its preamble:

> ...convinced that Africa's greatest resource is its youthful population and that through their active and full participation, Africans can surmount the difficulties that lie ahead.

b. Agents of insecurity vs. agents of transformation

In traditional Worldview and Mindset approach, the youth are mobilised as agents of insecurity, with violent gangs and extremist groups recruiting them to serve their narrow interests – with the promise of utopia.

The Transformed Empowered Worldview and Mindset approach views youth as agents of transformation for their generation. They are *mobilised* and *empowered* as responsible citizens who build their society for a secure future.

c. Wild and uncontrollable vs. potential to be harnessed

In Traditional Worldview and Mindset approach, the youth are viewed as wild and uncontrollable people who need laws and regulations to control them. They have little participation in shaping the destiny of society and are only listened to through agitation and demonstrations. They are seen as idlers and rebels who trade in vanity and are opposed to all else around them – paying for it in the hard currency of wasted opportunity.

The Transformed Empowered Worldview and Mindset approach views the youth as embodied with great potential, skills and talents to be *harnessed*. Space is deliberately created for the youth voice to be on the table of dialogue and engagement. The youth are viewed – not as idlers – but as unengaged resources to be engaged in transforming society. They are not viewed as rebels, but as dynamic change agents who present the energy, passion and optimism that is needed in shaping a new reality for communities.

d. Passive recipients vs. captains of own lives

In traditional Worldview and Mindset approach, the youth are viewed as persons who should be passive recipients of what is put on the table for them. Decisions are made on their behalf such that even when good intentions are on the fore, the interpretation of what is good for youth is made for them. They remain on the periphery of issues and are perceived as passive adapters of what others have processed for them. For example, they often serve as political youth wingers to help others ascend to leadership – with the promise of their issues being addressed. They never are!

The Transformed Empowered Worldview and Mindset approach views the youth as captains of their own lives and champions of community transformation. They are *active* drivers of their own change process and provide *leadership* in their spaces. They are the decision-makers and are actively engaged in finding that which is good for society. In this framework, the youth are not seen as passive adapters of what others have processed, but are catalysts of sustainable transformation. The youth should not just be spectators of the goings on in their country but must be involved in shaping the leadership and direction of their nation.

e. Leaders of tomorrow vs. leaders today

The traditional Worldview and Mindset approach regards the youth as leaders whose time has not yet come. Programmes are designed to focus on building their capacity for leading in the future. They are perceived as inexperienced and not capable of comprehending the issues of the moment.

The Transformed Empowered Worldview and Mindset approach views the youth as leaders today, fully competent and qualified to engage societal challenges that need addressing. They are solution seekers for challenges facing the society – much as Joseph did in Egypt and Jesus did for the world. They are seen as presenting new perspectives of looking at challenges and injecting entrepreneurial acumen in the life of the community.

The table below shows the level of participation of the youth in community life. Real development must focus on the youth in the country and bring them into the conversation around development. It is not enough for them to be on the forefront of fighting for change, they must be in the driving seat of change and progress of their nation.

Table 11.6: Political participation by age category in selected sub-Saharan countries, 2005–2006

Country	Attend community meeting			Raise issue			Attend protest demonstration		
	Youth	Elderly	Diff.	Youth	Elderly	Diff.	Youth	Elderly	Diff.
Benin	48	62	-14	31	43	-12	12	12	0
Botswana	57	82	-25	55	59	-4	19	17	2
Cape Verde	38	33	5	41	30	11	15	5	10
Ghana	46	62	-16	44	54	-10	9	6	3
Kenya	59	81	-22	54	68	-15	14	12	3
Lesotho	65	92	-27	51	77	-26	4	3	1
Madagascar	88	93	-5	66	74	-7	15	12	3
Malawi	81	79	2	34	39	-4	10	5	5
Mali	48	67	-20	22	38	-16	7	6	1
Mozambique	71	80	-9	65	73	-8	20	25	-5
Namibia	45	71	-26	26	49	-23	13	25	-13
Nigeria	42	63	-21	39	57	-17	15	17	-3
Senegal	59	67	-8	41	48	-7	16	15	1
South Africa	55	63	-7	42	47	-5	26	25	1
Tanzania	73	86	-13	61	75	-13	14	18	-4
Uganda	72	87	-15	57	72	-15	10	10	0
Zambia	57	72	-15	38	48	-10	10	10	0
Zimbabwe	54	75	-21	50	60	-11	10	7	3
Mean	59	73	-14	45	56	-11	13	13	1

Source: Chikwanha and Masunungure (2007).

f. Objects of abuse vs. a future to be nurtured

The traditional Worldview and Mindset approach views the youth as a captive market for fulfilling narrow and retrogressive interests of drug and substance abuse and other societal vices. Those who are engaged in these vices are often written off as failures, people who amount to less than nothing.

The table below shows the percentage of students who drank at least one drink containing alcohol.

Table 9.1: Percentage of students who drank at least one drink containing alcohol on one or more of the past 30 days, in countries of WHO regions, various times frames in 2003–2010 period

WHO member	Male (%)	Female (%)
Benin	18.2	12.5
Botswana	22.8	18.7
Ghana	26.4	29.3
Kenya	16.8	12.3
Malawi	5.3	2.5
Mauritius	19.3	16.8
Morocco	5.5	1.6
Namibia	35.0	30.9
Senegal	4.0	2.0
Seychelles	62.1	61.2
Swaziland	19.6	14.3
Uganda	14.1	11.6
Zambia	38.7	45.2

Source: WHO (2011a).

The Transformed Empowered Worldview and Mindset approach views the youth as the future of society, to be nurtured and protected. The youth represent the promise of the future and sustainability of any development initiatives.

Efforts are made to facilitate *rehabilitation* and *transformation* of the youth, who may have been caught up in the web of drug and substance abuse – and other vices – and mobilizing them as agents of transformation.

g. More mouths to feed vs. more hands to produce

The Traditional Worldview and Mindset approach views the swelling youth population as a challenge of more mouths to feed. Their swelling population is seen as a challenge to be overcome as it puts a strain on resources and reduces per capita. Preoccupation is placed on how to control population growth, to stay within the available resources. This is captured in initiatives such as the *panga uzazi* campaign in Kenya. Here is a picture of youth growth in Kenya:-

Year	Youth Population (15-34 yrs old)
1969	3,324,138
1979	4,943,037
1989	7,070,815
1999	10,181,521
2009	13,665,378

Source: Various Kenya Population Census Reports

Unless efforts are made to empower the youth now, Kenya faces a huge employment gap in which a small percentage of the population carries the burden of the rest of the nation.

The Transformed Empowered Worldview and Mindset approach views the swelling youth population as *more* hands to be engaged in production. It does not view youth population growth as a threat, but as a doorway to many possibilities, opportunities and markets. The youth are seen as receptacles of new solutions that the society needs. They are mobilised and equipped with skills and capacities to take charge of their destiny. These capacities include opportunities, spaces, resources and frameworks.

h. Treating symptoms vs. addressing root causes

The Traditional Worldview and Mindset approach focuses on programmes that help the youth address their *challenges* in isolated ways. Focus is made on such issues as responding to HIV-AIDS, unwanted pregnancy, addressing the FGM issue, and tackling early marriages that keep many youth away from school. In essence, this worldview focuses on symptoms and not the real issues the youth face.

The Transformed Empowered Worldview and Mindset approach seeks to build on programmes that focus on equipping the youth with life skills; building positive lifestyles that help the youth to experience life in its fullness. Under this mindset, for example, it is not enough to pursue abstinence programmes due solely to the challenge of HIV-AIDS, but out of convictions on *abstinence* as a value that society should embrace. The focus goes beyond symptoms to addressing real issues of the heart. *Behaviour* is linked to deep convictions that go beyond the mere fear of consequences and onto the commitment to be responsible and accountable to the author and giver of life.

Reflection
   a. Many governments and institutions are developing great plans on how to develop and empower the youth. There is one problem though. The youth are missing at the table. What will it take for policymakers to bring the voice of youth to the table? What will it look like to have the youth drive their agenda of development?
   b. From discussions on how the urban and rural youth are suffering from the *mwolyo* mindset, what strategies do governments, universities and educational institutions need to adopt in order to produce empowered youth who drive their own *destiny*, and *transformation* of their community?

8   CHAPTER EIGHT

SUSTAINABLE COMMUNITY SECURITY

East Pokot, in the North Rift region of Kenya, has been *known* for the constant insecurity associated with cattle rustling and an intense scramble for pasturelands. Even though there are other cultural and historical contributors to the roaring insecurities there, CIM has discovered that failure to develop alternative sources of income, especially among the restless youth, is a strong factor in this insecurity equation.

In an environment where the youth are unengaged, and there's heavy reliance on rain, whose patterns are ever changing in the face of climate change; where cultural and social factors have diminished business options, community vulnerabilities have been accentuated. Some of the challenges faced by the youth in East Pokot include FGM, early marriages, dropping out of school, drugs and substance abuse and unemployment.

The hope for East Pokot, like many other places, is in *embracing* a transformed and empowered worldview and mindset. This should be a worldview that shifts focus from dependence to finding solutions that keep the youth engaged in wealth-creation through plugging into the production value-chains.

Daniel Ruto, from Korelach Village, East Pokot, was one of the members of a delegation that visited Yatta to learn how the CIM Development Model could be replicated in his village. Having seen the opportunities for youth, and value of water in spurring agricultural production, upon returning to Korelach Village, Ruto settled on a land, near Kerio River, and started using the water to irrigate his farm. From farming on an eighth of an acre, he expanded to one acre within six months. He grew tomatoes, kales, onions, maize, green grams and water melons – using the 1-Acre-Rule Miracle.

Since starting this project, five other families have moved into the area to observe and learn from him. He has engaged a manager to help on the farm, with an additional workforce of fifteen other people. They help in providing orientation to those who visit his farm to learn.

Daniel Ruto has experienced what many families in Yatta have: *sustainable security*. We now know, based on our work in Yatta, that sustainable community security can never be possible when people are angry, hungry and hopeless. This is why, as Daniel began his work in East Pokot, we asked him to be true to his goal of creating sustainable development, and to be aware of what the components of such development are.

Components of Sustainable Development

For sustainable community development to take place, there are five key components that need to be addressed. They are:

- Structures
- Systems
- Vision
- Resources
- Leadership

These key components must operate right from the individual, to the household, village, local religious institutions, ward, constituency, county, diocese, country, region, continent and global levels. Because of their importance, we need to discuss each in-depth.

a. Structures

Creating and strengthening community structures, right from the village, requires great intention. These structures organise communities for more strategic engagement. They provide efficiency and coherence in how the community is to flow.

President Yoweri Museveni, of Uganda, created local councils in the village, a factor that contributed to placing Uganda on the road to recovery following years of unrest. Mwalimu Julius Nyerere, in Tanzania, created *Ujamaa* as a structure that helped create a new definition of nationhood. This helped the nation overcome the challenge of divisive ethnic politics. The table in next page illustrates the structures Nyerere put in place.

\	Tanzanian Example Population 44,928,923			
Region Equivalents	Name	Population 44,928,923	Political	Administrative
Nation	Nchi	30 mikoa	Rais	Rais
Regions	Mikoa	3-7 wilaya	Mkuu wa Mkoa	Mkuu wa Mkoa (Regional Administrative Secretary)- Katibu Tawala Mkoa)
Districts	Wilaya	6-30 kata	Wabunge	Mkuu wa Wilaya (Mkurugenzi wa wilaya)
Divisions (central govt. admin/ borders arbitrary)	Tarafa	5 katas	Afisa Tarafa	Afisa Tarafa
Wards	Kata	2-6 vijiji	Madiwani	Mtendaji Kata
Villages/ Streets-	Vijiji/Mtaa	4-8 vitongoji	Mwenye kiti wa kijiji	Mwenye kiti wa kijiji (mtendaji wa kijiji)
Sub-villages	Vitongoji	30 nyumba kumi		Mwenye kiti wa kitongoji
Sub-sub villages (security)	Nyumba Kumi	10 households		

b. Systems

Systems provide platforms and nexus for the smooth flow of resources and concert efforts for transformation. Right from the village, we should see village and county systems at play. Systems include communication, value systems, early warning systems, security systems, transport systems, agricultural value-chain system and all other relevant systems.

Colonial governments left in place the agricultural crop value-chain system. Over the years, commercial systems took the reins – with diminishing production. In Kenya, for example, when Jomo Kenyatta took over at independence, he *emphasized* agricultural crop value-chain with crops like coffee, tea, sisal, pyrethrum and wheat. As the years rolled, this approach was dropped as maximising profits became the focus.

CIM is engaged in the process of bringing back this concept of agricultural crop value-chain. We are challenging counties to find ecological crops – and industries – and match them with global markets and infra-structure; right from village.

c. Resources

Resource-mapping is critical for community development. County governments and nations must be *deliberate* in assessing their resources. The greatest resource is the people of Africa.

d. Vision

There should to be an inspiring vision of what people are becoming and where their destiny lies. African leaders have to move away from being in office to serve their own interests and focus on an enduring vision of what their villages, counties and countries are becoming. This vision needs to be a shared function in which people are mapping their destiny.

Some African nations are trying and are ahead. However, this process needs to be participatory and not a desk-top research by some consultants without ownership from the people. As our counties develop documents like the County Integrated Development Plan, the first question to ask should be: what level of participation has there been?

e. Leadership

Leadership is needed to connect all these key components of sustainable community development. The question is – what kind of leadership? Mzee Jomo Kenyatta gave a rallying call for Kenyans to pull together through the Harambee spirit. He adopted a concept used by builders of the East Africa Railway to give it the new meaning of a nation pulling together.

Through this effort, Harambee schools were built at locational levels across the country. Resources were mobilised to pay for education for local students and for students proceeding for further studies abroad.

Such leadership was also evident in the Presbyterian Church of East Africa (PCEA), when it made a painful decision to cut off reliance on donations from the West and declared a moratorium of self-reliance or JITEGEMEE. The result has been an economically empowered religious entity whose massive resources can be seen today.

Yatta has today evolved into a case study of how the OMO philosophy helped eliminate dependence and created self-reliance. CIM advocates responsive leadership at the county and national governments; religious institutions, UN bodies, universities and research institutions. Our desire is that leaders at these levels will embrace a posture that unites these five components in the pursuit of sustainable community development.

The UN piloted the tech villages, which, unfortunately, did not work. The reason they did not work was because they were donor-dependent and did not address the *mwolyo* mindset – as we have seen elsewhere in the book.

I end this segment by saying this – as our universities grapple with developing a curriculum that best addresses the needs of Africa, their efforts have neglected people's anthropological experiences and worldviews and may not yield much fruit. Any curriculum that fails to address the five core components in transformation is doomed to fail.

Key Questions in Comprehensive Community Security

One of the most critical challenges we faced when we arrived in Yatta was that of lack of security. This was, of course, to be expected because we had come into a land of hunger, where the only reliable means of survival was *mwolyo*. Under the circumstances, it was no surprise that village youth – and even starving adults – were tempted to find an alternative way, if only to boost their "earnings."

Like any reasonable human being, Agnes and I had to wonder how to regard the youth, our neighbours and even those with whom we mingled at daytime. Were they friends or foes? Were they a threat or an added layer of security?

a. Neighbours as a threat vs. neighbours as opportunity for collaboration

In Traditional Worldview and Mindset approach, neighbours are seen as a threat to progress and development. No efforts are made to build bridges and collaborate. This mindset is informed by a *scarcity mentality*, which holds the view that there are limited resources and only a few can access them. The resultant effect is conflict and a deliberate construct of barriers to isolate others and shield resources. Effort is made to eliminate competition as an unwanted element.

Transformed Empowered Worldview and Mindset approach views neighbours as an opportunity for collaboration and expansion of the market base. Efforts are made to build bridges and increase opportunities for collaboration. This mindset is informed by an *abundance mentality*, which holds the view that there are enough resources for all. Deliberate plans are made to reach out to neighbours and forge synergies. Effort is made to encourage competition and to learn from it.

b. Disarmament vs. tackling root causes

In Traditional Worldview and Mindset approach, focus is placed on disarming communities in conflict without any commitment to tackling the root causes of the conflict. There is low capacity for alternative conflict resolution mechanisms and disarmament only changes the type of weapons used, but does not address the conflict.

In Transformed Empowered Worldview and Mindset approach, focus is placed on tackling root causes of conflict and building capacity of the community to embrace alternative conflict resolution mechanisms.

In Yatta, as is the case all over Kenya, I have regarded failure to seek transformative solutions to people's problems as a modern form of witchcraft. Those who are wealthy, powerful and influential in society – with the capacity to pull the lowly out of perpetual misery, yet fail to do so – are no better than the sorcerers and witches of the yesteryears. Having a bank account that swells deep into the billions while your neighbours live in screaming poverty is not just corruption, it is *uchawi*. *Uchawi* is the Swahili word for witchcraft.

We can and must do better!

c. Fixedness on tradition vs. transforming tradition

In Traditional Worldview and Mindset approach, there is a high degree of fixedness and loyalty to tradition even when they have run their course and need to change. Interrogated deeply, some of these traditions are discriminative against sections of the community and are jealously guarded – and promoted by their greatest beneficiaries. This ultimately leads to a disempowered community that fails to build on synergies and adjust to unfolding realities.

In Transformed Empowered Worldview and Mindset approach, there is low degree of *fixedness* and loyalty to tradition – and enhanced commitment to reviewing and transforming traditions so that they can respond better to unfolding challenges.

Traditions that are considered discriminative against sections of the community are willingly reviewed by all, including their greatest beneficiaries. This builds an empowered community that builds on synergies and adjusts to unfolding realities.

d. Victim vs. *utongoi*

The Traditional Worldview and Mindset approach exhibits a victim mentality that promotes the *mwolyo* mindset of dependency. Elements of vulnerability in the community are given loud pronunciation, which projects the community as passive recipients of help and support. Such strategies as cash transfers are used to maintain the vulnerable in the community on a *lifeline*, without a strong commitment to build business and entrepreneurial acumen.

In Transformed Empowered Worldview and Mindset approach, communities exhibit a leadership or *utongoi* mentality in which they *perceive* themselves as leaders in driving their own development agenda. They engage other partners but perceive themselves as ultimately responsible and accountable for their development. Efforts are made to build the capacity of communities in *generating* resources and enhancing business and entrepreneurial acumen.

e. Threat vs. opportunity

The Traditional Worldview and Mindset approach views competition as a threat. Efforts are made to frustrate others and to operate with a high degree of secrecy. There is heavy reliance on vices such as witchcraft and Spiritism for personal gain – and social and spiritual advantage.

In Transformed Empowered Worldview and Mindset approach, competition is seen as an opportunity for improvement and continuous learning. Significant weight is placed on learning from others, in ways that inform various interventions. This mindset operates on the belief that one's destiny is secure; that it possible for all to succeed. Spiritual formation leads to servant leadership for the benefit of all.

f. Mbokisi vs. foresight

In Traditional Worldview and Mindset approach, there is a boxed-in thought process in which no learning takes place in relation to past experiences. This is captured by what I earlier described as *mbokisi* – a Kamba derivative for having a narrow and unproductive mind. Despite changes in weather patterns, for example, this mindset sticks to the same farming habits and patterns that no longer work.

In Transformed Empowered Worldview and *Mindset* approach, there is foresight and insight to stay open to opportunities around and beyond. The community exhibits a teachable spirit and uses the lessons learnt in its own life and growth. The mindset remains alive to changing realities such as weather patterns and embraces appropriate technologies and approaches in charting its destiny.

g. *Fogothary* vs. systematic approach

In Traditional Worldview and Mindset approach, there is a random, segmented and haphazard manner of handling development. This is best captured as *fogothary* – a slang word in the Kenyan context that means lack of a plan and order. It is a mindless execution of programmes and initiatives.

In Transformed Empowered Worldview and Mindset approach, there are known systems and structures for guiding development. Leadership is engaged in facilitating the smooth functioning of systems and structures. In this mindset, there is a systematic and logical construction between water security, health security, food security, spiritual security, social security, political security and economic security of the community.

The mindset recognises that each of these aspects is necessary for delivering sustainable community security. Political security helps to develop policies, legislations and regulations that either empower or *disempower* communities.

Spiritual security provides a framework for values and beliefs that either liberate and empower communities or hold them captive to such vices as witchcraft, animism and fatalism. Financial security helps to foster a village's economic zones, which builds livelihoods and creates assets on the value-chain.

Sustainable community security must address the holistic needs of communities in which their physical, social, spiritual and other-community interconnectedness needs are integrated.

Key Elements of Comprehensive Community Security
a. Water
Water is a significant component in community development. In the wake of climate change threats, an adaptation is needed in how water is accessed, utilised and conserved. Water harvesting techniques are needed to ensure there is a deliberate shift from rain-fed agriculture to irrigation agriculture, and that it is done in a manner that's sensitive to multiple water uses.

This calls for *leadership* that mobilises communities to undertake such initiatives as digging of water pans, zai pits and trenches. These initiatives will mitigate flush flooding and run-off that is common in ASAL areas. They will also reduce demand on underground water reservoirs and make available potable water with low salinity in some of the areas.

b. Food security
Food security means the whole gamut of availability, access and utilization – and all factors that affect these three areas. Resources are needed for production, for food to be available. Even then, income levels and *consumption* are critical elements of access, while nutritional needs and overall health are critical components of food utilization.

Sometimes the commercial interests are at the expense of food security in an area. Efforts are needed to ensure communities are being facilitated to be food-secure through interventions such as access to farming inputs like quality seeds, appropriate breeds and farm extension services.

Consider the following figure that highlights rainfall patterns and different livelihood clusters in Kenya. There is a strong correlation between rainfall patterns in the country and the livelihood clusters. The clusters demonstrate a high reliance on rain-fed agriculture.

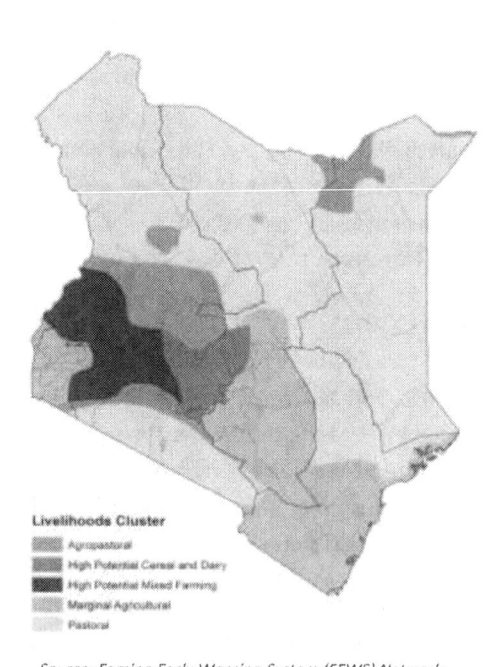

Figure: Livelihood Clusters

Source: Famine Early Warning System (FEWS) Network

Through irrigation and other climate change threat adaptation, it is possible to integrate the livelihoods above in which the pastoralists also engage in agriculture.

c. Health

Some of the challenges facing communities have to do with the distance covered to access nearest health facilities. Through advocacy and partnership with the government, religious institutions and other development partners, health facilities and qualified personnel need to be deployed to address preventive health and treatment.

d. Economic well-being

Through interventions like crop and animal value-addition programmes, *communities* will experience *economic boost*. Leadership is needed to mobilise the corporative movement that builds synergies in the community – and with other communities. The youth and women in these areas need to be integrated in the wealth-creation and wealth-control equation.

e. Koinonia

Koinonia is community-building in which relationships are enhanced and efforts are made to deescalate tensions that sometimes exist due to resource access and utilization conflicts. For pastoralist communities, major conflicts revolve around water and pasturelands.

f. Spiritual

True community-building must bring on board people's values, beliefs and core convictions. It must work with them in a transformative manner. Religious institutions have a significant role in the life of a nation.

Dependence Syndrome or The *Mwolyo* Mentality

Mwolyo is a Kamba word that means relief. It is often used in reference to food rations, which people line up to receive in case there is famine or drought. It has, for a long time, been a common feature due to unreliable rainfall patterns. *Mwolyo* has become embedded in the culture of the Akamba.

The *mwolyo* culture has brought about an *unhealthy* dependence. Indeed, according to us, it is anything one receives that he or she has not worked for. We refer to this as the *mwolyo* mentality or *dependency syndrome*. With this mentality, no one can develop. Whoever seeks to help anyone with this problem – without getting rid of the *dependency software* – cannot succeed regardless of how much money he or she has.

Why We Fight Dependency

Dependency syndrome refers to an attitude and belief that a group cannot solve its own problems without outside help. It is a weakness that is made worse by charity.

I once visited a project of a famous organization working in Kenya. Officials there took us to an area in Ukambani, where they had been involved in digging water pans. From the report they gave us, they had dug six pans for six years. Of those six years, the pans had remained dry. This, we were told, was because funding dried up before they could dig the canals and spillway for water to drain into the pans.

I was deeply saddened by the thought that they had spent more than six million shillings per water pan, for six pans, which had no water, yet in Yatta we had more than 3000 pans that had water. The difference was that the people of Yatta had been empowered to know their needs and to know that they were in a position to handle them. Their destiny was in their hand!

Today, if an outside agency – be it the central government, an international NGO or a religious entity – came to a community and constructed a facility (e.g. water supply), it would be natural for community members to see it as belonging to the outside agency. When that outside agency goes away or runs out of funds, community members will have no motivation to repair and maintain the facility, or to sustain the service. I have heard of water pans being silted yet people have no water.

Dependency, we now know, impoverishes!

Own the Problem, Own the Solution

The problem is never money or the water pans; the problem is the approach, the process. People need to own the process and the solution. In order for a facility to be maintained and sustained, community members must have *a sense of responsibility* for the facility. That sense of responsibility is described as *ownership by the community*.

Unless the community has been involved in decision-making about a facility – planning and management – and has willingly contributed time, energy and resources to its construction, a sense of responsibility or ownership will lack. The facility will not be effectively used, maintained or sustained. It is *impossible* to build a human settlement facility or service and not expect that it has to be repaired and maintained.

As we noted in a previous chapter, development is not just about structure, it is about sustainability of an effort. With proper engagement, people would own and run a facility even after a donor is gone. If not, it will just add on to the numerous white elephants, the many stalled projects that we have in our communities. They are good ideas that ended up badly.

Overstretched Central Pool

There's a new dynamic at play today. As populations grow, governments are getting access to fewer and fewer resources per capita every year. It is no longer feasible for communities to be dependent upon central governments for human settlement facilities and services. International donors like rich countries' governments, the UN, World Bank and international NGOs also don't have enough resources to give to every poor community, no matter how worthwhile the cause is.

In the past, community self-reliance was thought to be a good thing. It promoted grassroots democracy, human rights, self-development and human dignity. I believe this remains true even today if communities are helped to organise for self-reliance and transformation. If communities do not become self-reliant and empowered, they will not develop. Poverty and apathy will eventually destroy them.

Aiding to Fail

The desire by Western nations and organisations to see Third World countries reached and developed cannot be described in any way other than a tremendous display of philanthropy and concern for humanity. Many times, they are called upon to bring relief in a season of disaster, drought or famine and they answer the call. This is a remarkable gesture for which we need to acknowledge and appreciate our friends from the West.

I believe, however, that Africans have been made poorer by constant dependence on aid. But relief should not be confused with development. Relief implies a temporary state and no relief agency should establish a permanent presence. Our goal should be getting our people to a place of self-dependence and sustainability. We should take off the mantle of relief work and put on the mantle of being agents of empowerment and transformation. Anyone who promotes dependence on relief, in whatever magnitude, is paralyzing the potential for growth and development and that, in itself, is equivalent to *witchcraft*.

Referring to the effect of aid in the third world, Graham Hancook says it (aid):

> ... has sapped the initiative, creativity and enterprise of the ordinary people and substituted the superficial and irrelevant glitz of imported advice, it has sucked potential entrepreneurs and intellectualism of the developing countries into non-productive *administrative* activities; it has created a moral tone in the international affairs that denied the hard task of wealth creation and that substitutes easy handouts for the rigors of self-help; in addition, throughout the third

world, it has allowed the dead grip of officialdom to suppress popular choice and individual freedom.

I believe no one should be heard saying: *I worked in that community until my retirement and so and so took over from me.* In OMO, we refer to that as *mbokisi*, which means *not thinking*, behaving as if your head were *an empty box*. Any people we work among must be left looking to the future with a smile and not to us with a frown.

Our mandate is to help paint a picture of a better future and walk with them towards that future by helping them identify the existing challenges and work out an exit strategy from the present challenges. This is my definition of genuine capacity-building. Most organisations have funding *specifically* designated for this purpose, so I believe it can be done.

Competition Turned on its Head

One day, as I drove from Nairobi to our rural home, I met a jovial woman who was a member of a local Community Based Organisation. At the time, I was Chairman of the Board of Governors. She was thrilled to see me. She burst into praises, saying I was a man who always said the truth. She went on to narrate how a goat had been given out at the CBO to go to the *poorest* and, for some reason, she didn't get it. According to her, she deserved it because she considered herself as the poorest of the poor. She was at the bottom of the pile!

Can you imagine people having to fight for the title of being the poorest? It is because we have conditioned them to believe the so called *most vulnerable and poor* are the ones who end up getting any kind of assistance.

It should, therefore, not surprise anyone that people are *working hard* to win the coveted title of *most poor and vulnerable* from development agencies. It is cutthroat competition. Competition turned on its head.

Self-Esteem

It is important to always encourage community members by affirming that they have the ability to carry out a project by themselves. You are only there to offer skills and tips, but the work must be done by them. It ought to be clear that their situation is temporary. The poor *today* can be the rich *tomorrow*. They must know we are here to help them. Our goal is to help boost their self-esteem.

Self-esteem is a term used in psychology to reflect a person's overall evaluation or appraisal of his or her worth. It *encompasses* beliefs (for example, "I am competent") and emotions such as triumph, despair, pride and shame. It is expressed in: self-worth, self-regard, self-respect, self-love – which can express overtones of self-promotion – and self-integrity. Self-esteem is distinct from self-confidence and self-efficacy, which involves beliefs about ability and future performance.

For self-esteem to grow, we need to have self-worth, and this self-worth will be sought by embracing challenges that result in showing successes.

In CIM's OMO, we have adopted this theory in our slogan, which also embodies the spirit of our philosophy. It has three components:

- Sovereignty of God as the one who gives us power to make wealth (Deuteronomy 8:18).
- Our call to dominion as *atongoi* or leaders.
- Our desire and commitment to be self-sustained.

Reflections

a. In most parts of Africa, agricultural crop value-chain system that is used is that which the colonial master left with us. Why has it not been possible for many of these nations to attain food security?

b. CIM is bringing back this concept of agricultural crop value-chain and is challenging counties to find *ecological* crops and industries – and match them with global markets and infrastructure right from the village, ward, constituency and county. What will this look like in your context?

c. How can the five core components of sustainable community development be utilized in converting villages into agriculturally commercial villages?

d. How can the UN and other development bodies *redesign* the concept of millennium villages to avoid the *mwolyo* mindset?

e. What will the experience of Yatta mean for a county government seeking to leave an enduring mark in the community?

CHAPTER NINE

QUALITY ASSURANCE

The nature of this chapter makes it necessary for us to open it with two *significant* scriptural texts. The first is Isaiah 65:17-26 (KJV).

> ¹⁷ For, behold, I create new heavens and a new earth: and the former shall not be remembered, nor come into mind.
>
> ¹⁸ But be ye glad and rejoice forever in that which I create: for, behold, I create Jerusalem a rejoicing, and her people a joy.
>
> ¹⁹ And I will rejoice in Jerusalem, and joy in my people: and the voice of weeping shall be no more heard in her, nor the voice of crying.
>
> ²⁰ There shall be no more thence an infant of days, nor an old man that hath not filled his days: for the child shall die an hundred years old; but the sinner being an hundred years old shall be accursed.

²¹ And they shall build houses, and inhabit them; and they shall plant vineyards, and eat the fruit of them.

²² They shall not build, and another inhabit; they shall not plant, and another eat: for as the days of a tree are the days of my people, and mine elect shall long enjoy the work of their hands.

²³ They shall not labour in vain, nor bring forth for trouble; for they are the seed of the blessed of the LORD, and their offspring with them.

²⁴ And it shall come to pass, that before they call, I will answer; and while they are yet speaking, I will hear.

²⁵ The wolf and the lamb shall feed together, and the lion shall eat straw like the bullock: and dust shall be the serpent's meat. They shall not hurt nor destroy in all my holy mountain, saith the LORD.

The second is Ecclesiastes 3:1-8 (KJV).

To everything there is a season, and a time to every purpose under the heaven:

² A time to be born, and a time to die; a time to plant, and a time to pluck up that which is planted;

³ A time to kill, and a time to heal; a time to break down, and a time to build up;

⁴ A time to weep, and a time to laugh; a time to mourn, and a time to dance;

⁵ A time to cast away stones, and a time to gather stones together; a time to embrace, and a time to refrain from embracing;

⁶ A time to get, and a time to lose; a time to keep, and a time to cast away;

⁷ A time to rend, and a time to sew; a time to keep silence, and a time to speak;

⁸ A time to love, and a time to hate; a time of war, and a time of peace.

I don't need to tell you how hard it was to move a people previously dependent on *mwolyo* from that mindset to a new mindset of – not just hard work – but efficiency while at it. In the early days of our community meetings, this was one of the subjects we dwelt on, stressing the *centrality* of doing everything with a touch of seriousness and utmost dedication. We were aware that if the farms were not well-prepared, our farm yields would not be of the highest quality and the Yatta exports would not be of the standards expected in the global community. This would make us not meet our set goal of ridding ourselves of relief aid.

I testify here that when the Lord is leading, things happen much faster than one can imagine. It didn't take long for the farmers in Yatta to catch the drift and work at efficiency. The first harvest we experienced might as well have been from some of the best farms in Europe or the United States. We didn't have the infrastructure for massive exports, but we were well on our way to becoming *exporters* of agricultural products. And it all happened in less than a year!

I am tempted to ask again – why does it take donor agencies so long to dig a water pan? Why does it cost so much? And just why has the government failed to dig pans all over the lands of the East and North so that communities can be weaned off of relief aid? What is taking so long? But we must stay focused on the subject matter of this chapter.

Elements that Define Quality

One cannot talk about quality assurance without talking briefly about its history. Global concern for quality is said to have sprung out of the Second World War. After that world war, industrial manufacturers in Japan produced poor quality items. This led to training in quality processes, which led to quality control. Later, the concept of *total quality* came up in the 70s. It looked at business processes running across an organisation. This is a deeply calibrated history, but it will suffice.

Students of management will recognise the following points as key elements that define quality management:

a. **Management should be in the *driving seat* of the process and lead from the front.** It includes keeping time and honouring each promise. Management has to lead the way in the process of quality assurance.
b. **Continuous capacity-building in the elements of quality.** This includes regular, preferably quarterly, trainings that aim at changing attitudes, equipping with

relevant skills, teaching principles, imparting knowledge, and availing technologies relevant for superior products.

c. Aiming at value addition and customer satisfaction. Quality is not quality unless the customer is satisfied.

d. Metrics. This includes keeping data and measuring against data. The systematic approach to development, under the CIM Model, seeks to entrench this principle. Data should be kept, and it should serve as a basis for decision-making. Participants on the agricultural value-chain should be helped to develop the right metric and trained to measure appropriately.

e. Commitment to continuous improvement. The CIM Development Model advocates continuous *improvement* and learning.

f. Quality commitment becoming the core culture of an organisation and owned by all. While management offers leadership, everyone involved in the value-chain must be committed to quality management.

Quality Assurance through Lenses of Worldviews:
a. Selective treatment vs. comprehensive

In the Traditional Worldview and Mindset approach, quality assurance focuses on the product. It neither interrogates the processes that lead to the product nor the impact created in the community.

The Transformed Empowered Worldview and Mindset approach views quality assurance as an opportunity to focus, not just on the end product, but on the process that led to the product – and their immediate and long-term impact in the community.

b. Static vs. dynamic quality assurance

In the Traditional Worldview and Mindset approach, quality assurance is limited to standards that were established in the past and that may have become obsolete. It does not take into account new advances in knowledge and tools.

In the Transformed Empowered Worldview and Mindset approach, quality assurance is dynamic and is committed to continuous improvement and learning. Lessons learnt are integrated into improving quality and setting up new standards to match environmental changes.

c. Who measures quality?

In the Traditional Worldview and Mindset approach, quality is measured by a few people, often experts from the cities. The language used in quality assessment is often technical and cannot be comprehended by the very people who need to ensure that quality is delivered in processes and in the products.

In the Transformed Empowered Worldview and Mindset approach, quality is measured as a collective corporate action. *Everyone* is involved in the quality assessment process. The technical language is put in a manner that can be understood by all and there is a platform for continuous feedback and improvement.

d. Output vs. impact

In the Traditional Worldview and Mindset approach, quality is measured only in terms of output, without regard to whether there was actual production or not. Such output includes aspects such as mobilisation of the community, conducting of training programmes and hosting participants on model projects. These processes could sap all the productive energy and leave the programme weak. Evaluation of quality is focused on the separate projects and programmes.

In the Transformed Empowered Worldview and Mindset approach, quality is measured in terms of outputs and actual impact. It is not enough to have such outputs as mobilisation of the community, conducting of training and hosting participants on model projects; these must lead to increased productivity in the community. For example, care is taken to ensure that the traffic of visitors to the model projects does not injure but enhances the productive life and tempo of the projects. Evaluation goes beyond individual projects and programmes and focuses on the value-chain.

Quality Assurance in the CIM Model

It has taken a long time for the CIM quality assurance model to evolve, but we are now at a point where it seems effortless. The farmers we have trained – and all those who serve at the farm with us – have inculcated in them the mindset that in everything they do, they go for nothing but the highest quality.

They are seeking nothing but the best. Because of the need to maintain the highest standards, we have divided our quality assurance approach into steps.

Step 1: Mobilising for mindset change factors

The following will be monitored at this stage as key elements of quality assurance:

- That the community is taken through a process in which it *interrogates* its culture and worldview as factors that may or may not be hindering its core development agenda.
- That cultural issues and mindsets, including animism and fatalism – which hinder personal initiative for *progress* and *development* – are addressed in mobilisation.
- That mobilisation is addressing religious and cultural beliefs that have a bearing on the understanding of poverty.
- That there is a mindset change which has confronted a reality where the community is accustomed to things being done for it. It is a mindset that believes the government, the NGOs, and other structures are the gatekeeper of development in a community rather than what they really are – catalysts.
- That through this *mindset change training*, communities are helped to develop a healthy understanding of the role of gender in development; and that households are mobilised as leadership units in which every person should be celebrated and given a chance to contribute to the well-being of the household.

Step 2: Mobilising for mass water harvesting for domestic and agricultural use

The following are monitored at this stage:

- That water is harvested for multiple use – including livestock, domestic and irrigation needs.
- That efforts and synergies are developed at household and community level to harvest and manage water.
- That efforts are made to embrace climate change *adaptation* in relation to how water is used to conserve soils, irrigate plants, feed livestock and meet domestic needs in an efficient and effective manner.
- That water-harvesting is done in ways that mitigate flush flooding and run-off that is common in ASAL areas. That it is done in ways that reduce demand on underground water reservoirs and makes available potable water with low salinity in some of the areas.
- That the digging of water pans is done in a way that leaves the surface for evaporation reduced; and that the water pan is positioned in such a way that it has an overflow valve or outlet; and that the inlet is not direct but goes through planned diversions that help reduce sedimentation in the water pan.

Step 3: Food security

The following are monitored at this stage:

- That farmers shall dedicate a section of land that would supply the staple food to the family.
- That the various technologies including zai pits, zero tillage or farming God's way, maize transplanting, drip

irrigation, and fertilizer or manure are used to realise food security.
- That not only has the size of land been maximally planned and utilized, but that the minimum land tillage method of ploughing – suitable for the soils in ASAL areas – is done. This is to avoid exposing soils to wash-off during the short but torrential rainfall that the area experiences. The wash-off normally carries away top soil, leaving the soil infertile, thin, gullied and gravely unproductive.

Step 4: High value crops

The following are monitored at this stage:
- That the high-value crops for a particular region are selected in partnership with centres of excellence and leading research institutions and colleges.
- That the project has grown to a level where it has a significant seed bank that is made available to other farmers in ASAL and other areas.
- That these high-value crops are planted in significant acreage and in a systematic manner as stipulated by the model. After food security needs have been addressed, the community is mobilised to adapt high-value crops for its livelihood needs. CIM believes the inclusion of this value-addition component at the center will go a long way in assisting to create market for the same and many other agricultural products produced by farmers in and around Yatta.

Step 5: Value-addition for wealth-creation

The following are monitored at this stage:

- That there is an accelerated economic platform by value-addition processes, designed to improve on farm produce and provide value proposition to customers in both value and price.
- That the community is mobilised to diversify its farm produce and integrate other relevant features like dryer, processing and packaging – at the *household* and *village* levels.
- That the value-addition shall include the elements of:

    A. Quality, that the product or service meet or exceed customer expectations.

    B. Functionality, that the product or service provide the function needed of it.

    C. Form, that the product is in a useful form.

    D. Place, that the product is in the right place.

    E. Time – that the product is in the right place at the right time.

    F. Ease of possession – that the product is easy for the customer to obtain.

- That through various value-addition processes, farm produce is generating more products than originally envisaged.
- That farmers are making maximum use of every item along the continuum of the four factors above: functionality, form, place, time and ease of possession.

Step 6: Development of agricultural, commercial and industrial villages based on major produce and products

The following are monitored at this stage:

- That the community is mobilised to move into cottage and commercial production.
- That there is a significant group of framers in the catchment area organised into *production* and *processing* units.
- That there is a high level of servant leadership that walks with the community to build win-win business programmes in which every member of the community comes out a winner.
- That structured dialogue and streamlined business engagement has become the norm.
- That entrepreneurs are given a chance to build business models in which raw materials and inputs are procured locally – with win-win efforts hinged not on individual level of effort but benefiting from the power of multiplied effort. The Yatta CIM Centre of excellence, through this model of growth, was set up and received support from partners to set up a bakery, a miller and a solar drier – and other technologies that are helping local communities.

Step 7: Market-linkage

The CIM Development Model seeks to ensure that appropriate market linkages are established. The model seeks to ensure:

- That the community accesses *credit* and *market linkages* needed to consume the surplus production.
- That the right infrastructure and policy framework is put in place to facilitate regional and international trade.
- That more emphasis is placed on capacity-building of the community to continue observing the quality assurance aspects as defined by the team and industry; as they drive the economic development of their households and community.

CIM believes that value-addition of local produce is the next frontier for local entrepreneurship. It should be the focus of any community involved in any form of Agriculture if the local producers are to benefit from their work. It is the lack of this aspect, in most communities' value chains, that has led to scenarios where everybody else seems to be making a kill from Agriculture – except farmers.

As many organisations and groups come to Yatta to study and learn from the CIM Development Model, my prayer is that it will go a long way in unlocking Africa's potential and turn her into a net donor continent.

Reflection

   a. In many circles, quality assurance has often been left to specialized institutions. How can this be changed so that the specialized institutions monitor quality, but those on the agricultural value-chain measure quantity?
   b. What role can the consumer community play in influencing quality dimensions through advocacy?
   c. How can the global market use its trade regimes to influence quality conversation?

CHAPTER TEN

MENTORING FOR TRANSFORMATION

On the nearly fourty-acre farm CIM runs for demonstrative purposes in Yatta, I always enjoy evening walks to reflect on the journey we have been on since getting to the place. I am humbled by what the Lord has accomplished through us in the short time we have been in Yatta, but more than that, I am deeply touched by the many lives we have turned around through an integrated mentorship programme that has not only focused on mindset change, but on change at an even deeper level – the heart. We have demonstrated that God has a lot to do with softening the ground for impactful transformation to take place by transforming the heart first.

I recall that when we first came to Yatta, we faced a people who were hungry, angry and hopeless. Among them were devil worshippers, sorcerers, night runners, and even wife beaters. The land was caught up in evil on a scale that could have made anybody flee in terror. Aware, though, that we had moved in to take control of a situation that had spiraled into a magnet for ridicule of Christianity and God, we rolled up our sleeves and went to war with Satan and his demonic cohorts. By any measure, this was a war for the hearts and souls of the people of Yatta. Looking back, I'm glad we started at that level.

In the years since, we have accepted the role of mentors, of those who – by our actions, word and thought – are passing on key lessons on life. Indeed, Agnes and I give glory to the Creator for enabling an environment where successful farming has been associated with blessings from a Higher Power rather than the whims of ancestors and cruel gods. In light of the integrated approach in successful farming and Christianity, we hold dear the conviction that *it is not just in what is being accomplished on the ground, but in what people are becoming.* Are our sons and daughters growing up in the fear of the Lord or are they beholden to worldly pleasures? Are our mothers and fathers aging in God or are they secretly lingering between the love of God and the love of demonic rituals?

A walk in Yatta – for those who knew the arid land before it became what it is today – unfolds the extent of transformation that has taken place in the mindset of the people. It reveals the capacity of man to turn life around. I believe, though, that transformation of the mind, if it is not accompanied by transformation of the heart, is a wasted opportunity. In the end, it will amount to nothing. This is the reason Agnes and I have remained committed to mentoring the Yatta community in all aspects of life – especially the spiritual. All our gains have had a strong foundation in God's favor and that's where we shall remain – at the foot of the cross!

Defining Mentoring

Mentoring refers to an environment of accountability in which the elements of goal-setting, learning and application is taking place. I have given you a brief overview of our approach to the matter, but it would be helpful to look at it through the lenses of the worldviews.

a. Programme vs. lifestyle

In the Traditional Worldview and Mindset approach, mentoring is seen as a programme to be taught in the classroom, with little practical experience. The objectives of the mentoring programme take precedence over the needs of the person being mentored.

The Transformed Empowered Worldview and Mindset approach views mentoring as a lifestyle to be demonstrated in the community. It goes beyond the mentoring programme and focuses on the person being mentored. The programme is reviewed and changed in order to best serve the interests of the person being mentored. The focus is on a lifestyle change, not mere acquisition of knowledge or skills.

b. Experts vs. practitioners

In the Traditional Worldview and Mindset approach, mentoring is seen as a preserve of *experts* with sufficient academic credentials. The programme is dependent on the experts, who are a few in number and who often, although they have great information, lack experience in applying that knowledge in practical ways. The Transformed Empowered Worldview and Mindset approach views mentoring as a platform for practitioners. It seeks to build on the *don't-just-tell-me-show-me* principle. It seeks to not only tell but to explain and demonstrate how it works, inspiring protégés for a lifelong impact.

c. Raising followers vs. *utongoi*

In the Traditional Worldview and Mindset approach, mentoring is centred on one person and it is focused on raising followers. Those followers continue being dependent on the expert and are incapable of replicating the programme without the help of the leader.

The Transformed Empowered Worldview and Mindset approach, on the other hand, views *mentoring* as an opportunity to reach many and multiply leaders or *utongoi*. These leaders are practitioners and actively help others to grow and practice that which is taught – and even raise other leaders. The process of multiplication keeps producing leaders who are in turn producing other leaders, ensuring perpetuity of the programme.

d. Theory Vs. Practice

In the Traditional Worldview and Mindset approach, mentoring is focused merely on knowledge acquisition. Focus is on information transfer and no effort is made to turn theories into practical experience. In essence, it raises "good" students who have understood theory and can reproduce it. Many *educational* systems have functioned at this level, being custodians of knowledge but failing to go beyond theory and provide practical application of such knowledge. The result is great research information that could change lives but no one is applying it. The Yatta approach is lacking.

In the Transformed Empowered Worldview and Mindset approach, mentoring focuses not only on theory but goes beyond and provides accountability systems and structures through which principles are applied. It seeks the application of knowledge to cause transformation. It focuses on leadership that is needed to operationalize systems and structures. It produces transformation models and *individuals* who put theory to work and are making a difference in their generation.

e. Teacher's world vs. student's world

In the Traditional Worldview and Mindset approach, mentoring process takes place in the world of the teacher. It pulls the student away from where action should be taking place. One common phenomenon is the scenario where NGOs run training programmes in big hotels yet targeting communities. Such an arrangement draws community members away from their world into a utopic environment that is removed from their reality, making it hard for participants to reconcile the lessons learnt with their context.

The Transformed Empowered Worldview and Mindset approach seeks to mentor in the world of the student. Training and other programmes are field-based, with immediate application of principles being taught. This action-centred learning is designed to add value to the community and build a sense of ownership.

f. Dualism vs. integration

In the Traditional Worldview and Mindset approach, mentoring is done in a disjointed format, with focus placed on a few areas such as field productivity. This is done without regard to such areas as the operational culture and the processes behind such productivity. If these areas are not addressed, injury to long-term productivity could result. In this case, *mentoring* is regarded as a job and as a vocation with limited scope – one that can be abandoned or taken up at will.

In the Transformed Empowered Worldview and Mindset approach, mentoring is done in an integrated manner, in which the focus is on total transformation. It addresses not only productivity but also the prevailing culture and systems – and related processes that have a direct impact on long-term productivity. Mentoring is seen as a calling not an assignment. It is regarded as a calling that goes beyond *the call of duty* and in which all elements are integrated to leave an enduring impact.

Key Elements in Mentoring

a. Choose people with great potential for a mentoring programme

People with great potential shall be chosen. They should be people with a desire to make a difference or have the potential to make a difference. There are people who are not exposed to transformation and may be at the bottom of the ladder, but their gifts and qualities display potential for improvement.

Moses was advised to choose able men out of Israel and make them heads over the people of Israel (Exodus 18:25). The wisdom to choose men of ability is a precursor to unparalleled success. Niccolo Machiavelli said:

> The first method for estimating the intelligence of a leader is to look at the men he has around him.

b. Set a climate of teamwork

A leader whose view is to ensure transformation, through trans-visioning, will create a supportive climate of trust. He who trusts one will entrust him with certain challenges, but make cushioning provisions for possible failure. If an organization encourages teamwork – with the authority line well drawn – everyone will have the opportunity to shine.

Nehemiah was such a transformational leader who allowed teamwork for the transmission of experience among the various groups assigned various jobs in the reconstruction of the gate of Jerusalem. Here is his brief account:

> The valley gate repaired Hanun, and the inhabitants of Zanoah; they built it, and set up the doors thereof, the locks thereof, and the bars thereof, and a thousand cubits on the wall unto the dung gate (Nehemiah 3:13, KJV).

c. Vision sharing or trans-visioning

Trans-vision is the ability of the leader to pass his vision to others. It is easy to attract followers, quite another thing to develop leaders who can move communities and institutions to higher levels. This is *transformational leadership*, where a leader develops his followers into disciples, then to leaders. It takes a sincere leader to grow other leaders.

There are two types of visions: spiritual vision and natural vision. A spiritual vision is a divine interpretation of what God wants done. Natural vision occurs at those times when the human ear hears from research or declarations or conventions of what needs be done. Moses – on the mountain – received a vision of how to make a sanctuary and these were God's comments, recorded in Exodus 25:8-9 (KJV):

> And let them make me a sanctuary; that I may dwell among them.
> 9 According to all that I shew thee, after the pattern of the tabernacle, and the pattern of all the instruments thereof, even so shall ye make it.

A vision has the ability to ignite passion and drive people to new frontiers. It lengthens people's sights to see the regions beyond, possibilities out of impossibilities and find a way in the wilderness. With great passion and vision, the preachers of the yesteryears saw beyond their parishes, way beyond their home districts. Examples abound of such men:

- William Carey, who saw the world and later landed in India – with educational limitation, with lack of travel documents, and without adequate sponsorship.
- Martin Luther saw faith-based salvation when everyone else saw the pope.

- Henry Marilyn saw the Muslim world of Persia and Arabia while his contemporaries were involved in some petty, theological concerns.
- Martin Luther King Jr announced his big dream that one day the Negroes would be free. He might not have lived to see that day, but visions are living forces which outlive the vision carrier.

The children of Issachar were visionary leaders. Through them, we know that a visionary leader is one who knows what needs to be accomplished. Indeed, when a visionary leader arises, God stirs others to stand with him.

> And of the children of Issachar, which were men that had understanding of the times, to know what Israel ought to do; the heads of them were two hundred; and all their brethren were at their commandment (1 Chronicles 12:32, KJV).

When true vision emerges, old programmes are set aside; religious beliefs which do not tie in with the vision are cut off; self- serving programmes are abandoned in favour of the vision. Indeed, when true vision emerges, unimaginable goals are set, people begin to accomplish tasks in record time – what once took generations many years to accomplish.

The reason the so called prosperity gospel has prospered today, while the Lord's command and the great commission have been abandoned, is explained in lack of visionary leadership in religious institutions. John Maxwell offers five ingredients of *divine vision* as:

- A clear picture which acts as a map.
- A positive change that improves the present conditions by introducing God's Kingdom.
- A future focus that furnishes direction to the unseen future.
- A chosen people and time.
- Vision Execution - Mission.

Oswald Sanders weighs in on this matter:

> A vision without a task makes a visionary
> A task without a vision is drudgery
> A visionary with a task makes a missionary

In ending this segment, we need to take home the thought that he who has vision and does not convert it into an action plan is nothing but *a visionary*. If William Carey, Hudson Taylor, and Livingstone had conceived their visions and failed to go to India, China and Africa, respectively, their dreams would have turned to nightmares. We must move from vision to action if we are to make an impact in society.

Mission as a Factor in Mentoring

mission = vision + action

Mission is the *evidence-based obedience to the call from God*. This evidence is seen in the ability to initiate an action programme; for one who has a vision does not sit and wait for opportunities to fall like rotten mangoes from a tree, but shakes the tree for the ripe mangoes to fall for safe use.

Mission should not be seen through the lens of academic knowledge, but in the very application of the same. Mission is going to the mission field and causing interaction, interruption and intervention. He who does not interact may not be able to intercede or intervene on behalf of the poor, the captive, and the vulnerable. Jesus example of ministry is worth copying:

> And Jesus went about all the cities and villages, teaching in their synagogues, and preaching the gospel of the kingdom, and healing every sickness and every disease among the people.
> [36] But when he saw the multitudes, he was moved with compassion on them, because they fainted, and were scattered abroad, as sheep having no shepherd (Matthew 9:35-36, KJV).

The fulfillment of a vision is in the *mission* and the fulfillment of a mission is in an *action plan*. Jesus' ministry relied on obedience to the call. As we noted in Yatta, when mission activity takes place, details begin to unveil and momentum begins to build. Indeed, as one ventures to the mission field, the need once perceived in dreams emerges. This red-hot need builds a burden and the burden develops an in-built passion and fire to go over to the other side of the problem, which is fulfillment and satisfaction of a successful mission.

Mission is about meeting needs and subduing challenges. People without vision will move from one ministry to another, just because they or the ministry, or both, do not have a mission. He or she who has not discovered his or her God-given mission is a tourist or a window-shopper. He or she is lost or has disobeyed the vision God gave.

Partnership Development

Transformational leadership considers everybody doing what they are doing as a partner. It attracts those who have similar aspirations, not to dominate but to act as a servant leader. The building of *strategic partnerships* is instrumental to success in any enterprise. To get to where we are today, in arid Yatta, we have partnered with World Vision, USAID, and a number of other global and local organisations. Through it all, we have found out that two elements are necessary for success in partnership:

- The ability to identify collaborators in the mission; those who are within the scope of the mission and those without.
- Identification of those who can share their resources with you. The point is – those who have the intention of doing the same thing would *surrender* their resources if they were assured that their interests were taken care of. Frank talk on key matters may be necessary since development organisations have budgets for specific events. They have to write a report too.

Cultivating Prayer

A God-sized vision needs God-sized action. It drives us to rely on God more; and drives us to prayer. Prayer is the avenue through which we connect with God and His resources, for our lives and work. It is important that we walk with mentees and help them cultivate high reliance on God.

From Samuel Chadwick's biography we read:

> He was mighty in public prayer because he was constantly in private devotion.... When he prayed he expected God to do something. I wish I had prayed more, he wrote towards the end of his life, even if I had worked less and from the bottom of my heart I wish I had prayed better."

Prayer is an avenue through which we exchange our agenda with God's agenda for His people. It is one of the six means of grace God has put in place to cause growth in His children, others being:

- The word
- Fellowship
- Suffering
- Ministry opportunities
- Ministry of the Holy Spirit in the life of a community.

Prayer, therefore, is an avenue through which spiritual warfare is engaged in and communities liberated.

The significance and centrality of prayer in the ministry of our Lord Jesus Christ is demonstrated by His fourty days of *solitude* and frequent *withdrawal* before any decisive ministry throughout his three years of ministry.

- So he himself withdrew into the wilderness and prayed (Luke 5:16, NIV).

Later, there was Martin Luther. When he was asked about how he spent his day, he answered:

> Work, work from early till late. In fact I have so much to do that I shall spend the first 3 hours in prayer (Oswald Sanders, Spiritual Leadership. Lakeland, London. 1967, pg. 76).

Reflections

a. In your opinion, how can mentoring and coaching be institutionalized in a highly competitive capitalistic business environment?

b. What role could research institutions and centres of learning play in mentoring citizens in agricultural value chain?

c. What partnerships could be forged between religious institutions and the government in helping to develop mentoring and coaching programmes in agricultural value-chain at the grassroots level?

CHAPTER ELEVEN

PREPARATION FOR RETIREMENT

Let's get right to it. Regardless of how strong and gifted we are, retirement from employment is facing each of us as surely as day follows night. Many people in employment never see this coming and when the time finally comes to retire and give way for others, they are faced with the shock of a lifetime – *Where do I start from? What lifestyle changes do I need to make?* These are questions whose answers they don't have. Governments are also faced with an urgent burden in which those transitioning into retirement need support and upkeep from the insufficient pension schemes and overstretched and unemployed youth population. This is a crisis that is either happening now or is waiting to happen in many countries. Thankfully, the subject of retirement is viewed quite differently in the worldview and mindset lenses that we have been using.

Key Views on Retirement
a. Death sentence vs. new opportunity
In the Traditional Worldview and Mindset approach, retirement is considered by some as a death sentence, with

every effort made to avoid it. It is seen as the last stage before death, as a waiting room. This dire picture is *shaped* by how life has turned out for many people who've retired. They were psychologically unprepared to face their retirement phase. They were made to believe that their only preoccupation was to wake up, eat, and sleep. Homes for the elderly were developed in some contexts to put the elderly in special homes away from society and their family structures. To a large extent, retirement was packaged as the phase when diseases come home.

This is sad indeed!

Transformed Empowered Worldview and Mindset approach, on the other hand, views retirement as a new opportunity for growth and impact. It is an opportunity to try out new projects that one may have always wanted to do but there was no time. In a sense, this is the wise counsel Agnes and I adopted. We saw our coming retirement as an opportunity to learn and grow, but took the plunge when the dire situation in Yatta became intolerable to us. Yatta made us retire from formal employment earlier than we had planned. Retirement is seen as a stage of renewal and enjoyment of life through the wise choices made earlier. Life is faced and handled as it comes.

b. Pension focused vs. investment focused

The Traditional Worldview and Mindset approach is focused on consigning persons retiring to thinking in terms of pension. Pension is one of the greatest motivators for making career and employment options. Retirement is thus seen as a *spending phase,* a consumption stage with little production.

In the Transformed Empowered Worldview and Mindset approach, the focus is on building the capacity of persons retiring to diversify their investment options. It seeks to grow wealth in retirement and removes dependence on pension. Retirement is thus seen as an opportunity for increased production.

c. Accident vs. advance warning

Traditional Worldview and Mindset approach views retirement as an unwelcome accident. It comes upon many persons by surprise. Many people would wish to change their years if it were possible in order to continue being in public service.

In Transformed Empowered Worldview and Mindset approach, retirement is a joyous phase of life that should be prepared for adequately and resources and capacity built to engage at that level. Programmes are put in place to train and psychologically prepare the people to enter this phase. Such preparation should start right from the beginning of working years, but becomes critical at least five years before retirement.

d. Mob psychology investment vs. informed investment choices

In the Traditional Worldview and Mindset approach, persons preparing to retire are driven by the mob psychology of what is in vogue when acting on investment options. This is done with business feasibility studies, without a sound business plan. The result is such a crisis as has been in many rural parts of Kenya, where every retiring teacher retired with a posho mill. Soon everyone had a brand new posho mill in the neighbourhood, without enough space to drive business volumes. After one year, the businesses collapsed.

Transformed Empowered Worldview and Mindset approach allows for informed investment choices. Feasibility studies are done and proper business plans developed. Time and effort are put into building business acumen and accessing appropriate business resources and information. Investment is thus made gradually – over time – in order to test and refine the business model before retirement.

e. Expired vs. experienced

In the Traditional Worldview and Mindset approach, retired persons are viewed as having expired and they have nothing more to contribute. They are assumed to have passed their sell-by-date. In some cases, these very retired persons hold the same views about themselves.

The Transformed Empowered Worldview and Mindset approach considers retired persons as assets whose *experience* and wisdom is needed in moving society forward. Consequently, retired persons are moved into spaces and platforms that make maximum use of their many gifts and talents.

f. Fear vs. optimism

In Traditional Worldview and Mindset approach, retirement is handled with fear. The fear of uncertainty is so real for some people. Some feel retirement means loss of status, change in lifestyle and slow death.

Transformed Empowered Worldview and Mindset approach, on the other hand, views retirement as the opening up of a world of new possibilities. The retired persons maintain their sense of dignity and leverage on their experience in navigating their next curves.

The Fear of facing an uncertain future

At an individual level, many persons facing retirement are confronted with fear of the unknown and the uncertain. This has adverse effects on the health and wellbeing of individuals and could send some to an early grave. Some are known to use their pension to maintain their luxurious urban lifestyle and later retire to poverty and penury. So what steps should we take to prepare as individuals? As governments? As employers?

- **Preparation**

Five years before retirement, we need to start the preparation stages that make retirement bearable. These include exploring investment options, determining lifestyle changes needed to make it work, and determining appropriate locations.

- **Embracing Agriculture as an Option**

In a world where food security is still a challenge, agriculture will continue to be a great option for both the youth and the elderly population. It will give the seasoned professionals an opportunity for ploughing back skills and experiences.

- **Change of mindset about agriculture**

This calls for mindset change from the traditional white and blue collar jobs to tilling the land.

Donor Ourselves Philosophy

The *Donors Ourselves* philosophy is the key driver of Christian Impact Mission's transformation agenda. It is our contribution to the communities and nations of Africa and the world. What it engenders is the grand approach where we, as the leaders of new African development agencies, like CIM Trust, have come of age and may now become the new donor in Africa.

CIM focuses on the family and the individual as the basic unit of transformation. Transformation, in our case, targets *uplifting* of *an individual's* and *the family's* livelihood by effecting change in the way of life, attitude, and response to the environment. We focus on people's relationship with God and their community; and their willingness and ability to take the reins of their destiny. Through the *Donors Ourselves* philosophy, CIM Trust believes that as much as Africa and other 3rd world countries need external funding, we need to guard against any tendency of dependency syndrome.

As we now age, and have experienced the joy of farming in retirement, we see farming as the greatest initiative for wealth-creation that Africa has failed to tap into. Whereas CIM had projected to experience the programme's maturity in five years, it came much sooner and people took notice. This caused CIM to venture into training and replication sooner than had been earlier intended. Every stage of the ten point plan, which I discussed earlier, has thus been packaged into a transformation model that is easy to replicate.

The programme has received teams from major development agencies – and NGOs within the country. Among those we have welcomed are: World Vision Kenya, World Vision Tanzania, Norwegian Church Aid, Church World Service, Action Aid and Compassion International.

Operation Mwolyo Out has transformed Yatta from a land of men and women dependent on aid to a land of men and women who are donors. In retirement, Agnes and I have done vastly much more than we ever did in formal employment. The death of that mother was not for nothing – it started a movement. We dedicate the success of Operation Mwolyo Out to her memory!

Reflection

a. In your opinion, what is the appropriate time in the career of an employee to start talking about retirement? What elements should go into such a conversation?

b. Given the support burden that retirement is likely to visit upon a nation, what strategic interventions could governments take to prepare themselves and prepare their workforce in the face of impending retirement?

c. How could governments creatively find ways of developing structures which multiply pension schemes and help citizens to best face the uncertainties of the future?

d. How could agricultural value-chain offer the most sustainable retirement plan for the African working class? What policies will governments need to put in place to secure such a value-chain?

BIBLIOGRAPHY

Assensoh, A. B. *African Political Leadership: Jomo Kenyatta, Kwame Nkrumah, and Julius K. Nyerere*. Malabar, FL: Krieger Pub., 1998.

Blue, Ron. Storm Shelter: *Protecting Your Personal Finances*. Nashville: Thomas Nelson Publishers, 1994.

Buford, Bob. *Half Time-changing your game plan from success to significance*. Michigan: Zondervan Publishing House, 1994.

Delanyo Adadevoh. *Leading Transformation in Africa*. N.p.: ILF, 2007.

Drucker F. Peter. *The Effective Executive*. New York: Harper& Row, 1967.

Hancock, Graham. *Lords of poverty*. New York, Atlantic Monthly Press, 1994.

Handy Charles. *The Empty Raincoat. Making Sense of the Future*. London: Random House, 1994.

Jakes, T.D. *Reposition Yourself:- Living Life Without Limits.*
   New York: Atria Books, 2007.

Masika, Rev. *Titus. Triumph Through Disappointments!:
   Discovering God's Appointment in Your Disappointments.*
   Nairobi: King's Script Publishers. 2004.

Maxwell, John. *Developing The Leader Within You.* Malaysia:
   Printmate Sdn, Bhd, 1998.

Moyo, Dambisa. *Dead Aid: Why Aid Is Not Working and How
   There Is a Better Way for Africa.* New York: Farrar, Straus
   and Giroux, 2009.

Munroe, Myles. *In Pursuit Of Purpose.* Shippensburg: Destiny
   Image Publishers, inc., 1992.

Myers, Bryant L. *Walking with the Poor- Principles and
   Practices of Transformational Development.* New York: Orbis
   Books, 1999.

Nyerere, Julius K. *Freedom and Development: A Selection from
   Writings and Speeches 1968-1973.* Dar Es Salaam [u.a.:
   Oxford Univ., 1974.

Swenson, Richard A. *Margin: Restoring emotional, physical,
   financial and time reserves to overloaded lives.* Colorado
   Springs: Navpress, 1992.

Warren, Rick. *The Purpose Driven Life.* Grand Rapids,
   Michigan: Zondervan, 2002.

Website: www.wikipedia.org

ACKNOWLEDGEMENTS

In large measure, this book is the work of the many people who have played a big role – from inception of the idea to write an elaborate book that would summarize our lessons and experiences in Yatta and pass on these foundational lessons to other communities in Kenya and nations around Africa and the world.

A great sense of debt is owed to my wife and partner of many years, Agnes Masika. She has given great thought and reflection on gender issues and development and the whole area of family government in its design and function. Some of the chapters of the book carry her spirit and passion.

The Yatta community, especially Rev. Stephen Mwangangi and the leadership of Victory Life International Church Makutano, deserve special mention for their role in adaptation and advancement of the OMO philosophy and model.

Great appreciation goes to our children and the team that has worked with us in the various facets that now constitute the fundamental breakthroughs experienced in Yatta. It is not easy for members of a family to work together in mobilising communities towards community transformation, but God has been gracious with my family.

Jimmy Gor has played a great role in shaping the thinking of community mobilisation, team leadership and movement building. Together with Chris Wambua and Eunice Mulu, they have played a great role in giving attention to youth and young professionals' issues; and modeling the place of the youth in development. They are driving the agenda of securing the next generation and their lessons are invaluable.

Mercy Masika-Muguro has been instrumental in shaping the thinking of value-addition and product-development, including such projects as the bakery that is now producing Yatta bread, and other products.

Edith Mwethya played a key role in ensuring that systems and processes at the Yatta Model are put in place to support a fast-expanding movement of change in Africa.

Many people have played a great role in shaping the development model and we cannot exhaust the list here; suffice it to say that we are grateful to the many governments, religious institutions, community leaders, development agencies, and universities that paid us a visit to learn from us and to encourage us in our adaptation process.

Great appreciation to the communities and organisations that have taught us invaluable lessons as we modeled, taught, and mentored them in the implementation of the CIM Model, as first introduced and practiced in Yatta.

I am grateful to Christ Is The Answer Ministries (CITAM) for the immense support that we have received as CIM over the years, and the facilitation CITAM has played in helping to get this book written so that it might help many communities and nations.

Special mention to World Vision for walking with us during the implementation of the programme, and through whose facilitation we were able to train and mentor more than 1000 staff and community members – and government personnel in Tanzania, Kenya and Rwanda. We focused them on the CIM Development Model, especially the 1-Acre Rule Miracle.

Great appreciation to World Vision Rwanda, through which communities now have testimonies on how their eyes have been opened to see resources around them and to start using swamps as a source of water for irrigation.

USAID played a key role in supporting the implementation of the Kenya Horticultural Competitiveness Project, which helped to build the capacity of communities in potato growing and in setting up infrastructure needed for value-addition.

Great appreciation to Eric Wafukho, who has, over the years, stood with us in this development agenda and worked with the rest of the editorial team made up of Agnes Masika, David Saggia, Jimmy Gor and Edith Mwethya to provide flow for this book and ensure we summarised the lessons and experiences of our development journey.

Heartfelt appreciation to the great team at Sahel Publishing Association for believing in me. Through the leadership of Sam and Hellen Okello, you have published a world-class book. I thank God for your ministry.

Greatest acknowledgement is reserved to our God and Saviour, who alone takes credit for what He does through His people. May this book transform our lives and place us on a new path of progress and transformation.

Photo Gallery

Bishop Masika in his office at CIMCentre

A water pan construction in Yatta

Water harvesting

Wheat grass grown through moist bed technology

Chinese lettuce grown through aquaponics technology

Kales grown through aquaponics technology

Wheat Grass

Maize flourishing in Yatta

French beans

Bullet chillies

Pumpkin Farm

Pumpkin Harvest — *Sunflower*

Preparing ground for moist farming — *Kales on a moist farm at CIM Centre*

Organic Chicken

Geese and ducks, among the birds in the ecotourism

Ostriches   Bishop Masika feeding an Ostrich

Cows in their shade at the CIM Demonstration Farm

Bishop Masika presenting a certificate to one of the visitors at the CIM Centre

Toggenburg goats

Pig farming at the CIM Centre

Vermi composting

Rabbit shed as part of fish farming and aquaponics cycle

Fish pond also part of fish farming and aquaponics cycle

Sweet potato farm

Sweet potato harvest

Charcoal Cooler

Sweet potatoes in the charcoal cooler

Sweet potatoes in a grinder

Bishop Masika by the entrance of the Solar Dryer at the CIM Centre

Sweet potatoes in the solar dryer

Milling Machine   Sweet potato flour   Bread Mixer   Oven

Oven for baking

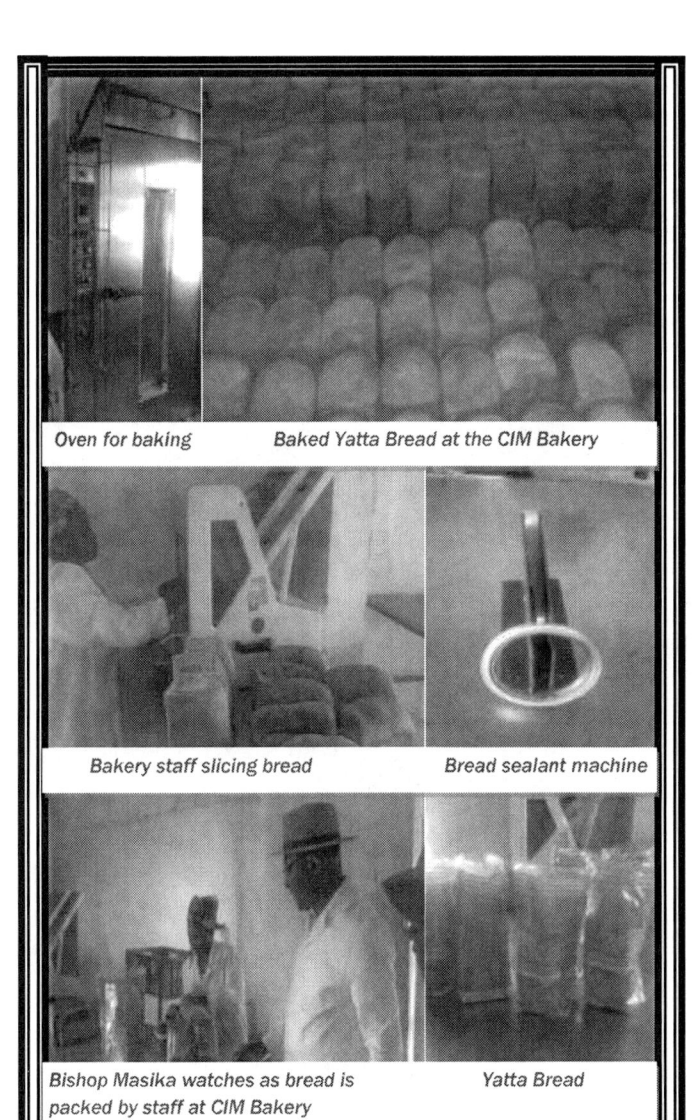

Baked Yatta Bread at the CIM Bakery

Bakery staff slicing bread

Bread sealant machine

Bishop Masika watches as bread is packed by staff at CIM Bakery

Yatta Bread

Bishop Masika at the CIM Shop

Yatta Honey and Cake, below

In the background, a water pan in Yatta

Soil testing equipment

Prof Musembi of University of Nairobi training on soil testing

Cabbages grown using drip irrigation

Ridges for planting sweet potatoes

Seedlings *Cabbage*

Visitors touring a demonstration farm in Yatta

Visitors at a demonstration farm

Bishops from Bondo visiting CIM Centre

Visitors at the CIM demonstration farm   *Peter at his farm*

Bishop Masika explaining the Mbokisi concept   *Visitors at CIM Centre*

The Deputy Makueni Governor and his staff at CIM Centre   *Rev. Agnes at a teaching session*

The Bakery   *Biogas processing*

The office complex under construction

Deputy Governor Machakos County, H. E. Bernard Kiala at the launch of CIM bakery and value addition plant

NGO - non-Governmental organization